HAPPINESS UNLIMITED

Self-Unfoldment in an Interactive World

HAPPINESS UNLIMITED

Self-Unfoldment in an Interactive World

Swami Bodhananda

Srishti
PUBLISHERS & DISTRIBUTORS

Srishti Publishers & Distributors
N-16, C. R. Park
New Delhi 110 019
srishtipublishers@gmail.com

First published by Sambodh Foundation

First published by Srishti Publishers & Distributors 2003

This impression 2011

Cover illustration: Nirmal Prakash

Cover design by Creative Concept

Typeset in AGaramond 11pt. Skumar at Srishti

CONTENTS

Introduction

Acknowledgements

1

Purity of Mind: *Antahkaranasuddhi*

25

Ways of Knowing: *Pramana*

53

The Enlightened Person: *Sthitaprajna*

79

Non–Reaction to the Fruits of Work: *Karma Yoga*

101

The Many Faces of God: *Sarvadharma Samabhavana*

121

Laws of Karma: *Karmasiddhanta*

151

The Spectacle of Change: *Mayavada*

177

The Ecstasy of Meditation: *Samadhi*

193

Appendices of Quotations

213

Ashrams & Organizations

INTRODUCTION

The architecture of this book, originally titled *Self-Unfoldment in an Interactive World*, is based upon three propositions, namely, 1) that the material objective universe is a manifestation of the invisible Universal Spirit; 2) that the beauty, splendour and power of the Spirit pours out through the complex processes of the mental and the material world; and, 3) that the Spirit fully actualizes in the conscious individual's choice-making and desire-fulfilling projects.

The Self is a dynamics of body, mind and Spirit. The body and mind are divisible and variable, whereas, the Spirit is indivisible and invariable. The first-person pronoun, 'I', refers to this Self. Thus, 'I' has reference to both the changing, phenomenal body-mind complex as well as to the changeless, inexhaustible Spirit. Self-unfoldment happens as the body-mind organizes, interacting with the environment, and becomes an integrated channel for Spirit's free expression.

This self-organization is accomplished when the individual pursues a worthy goal in life – like Beauty, Truth, Goodness, Justice, Equality, Compassion, Universal Love, Unconditional Happiness, or, the Paragon of All Virtues – God! Pursuit of these values is undertaken in an interactive world of work, amongst reciprocally cherishing and nourishing individuals. In the process, the primitive, egocentric conditioning of the mind loosens, and the individual's best interests are discovered to be served in a harmonious and engaging relationship with other individuals pursuing similar worthy goals.

The childish, neurotic individual matures to be a poised perceptive adult. An interactive life is a necessary precondition for cultivating maturity, mental purity and for responsible choice-making.

Further, an interactive life is necessary for the exploration and expression of an individual's potential – spiritual, mental and physical. The unconditional, unhindered realization of one's potential is the ultimate meaning of *samadhi* or Self-unfoldment. It requires emotional maturity, intellectual clarity, and physical and social wellness. In such a state of holistic perception, the God that we seek as a goal is understood as the innate potential of the goal-seeker. The more we express in an interactive world, the more we realize our Selves – the more we unleash our infinite power.

Self-unfoldment is the experience of individuals who dream, work and explore the limits of human power and potential – who expand and encompass the whole universe in all its depths and complexities, who synergize with a zillion points of individual brilliance and initiatives. This book is an invitation for those who seek immortality, not by dissolving into a lifeless homogeneity of a flat existence, but by becoming a vortex, a nerve centre of activities, gathering the might and splendour of the Spirit into their individual dynamism, coaxing the Spirit to awaken its fullness in manifold beauty into a multi-verse of heterogeneity – from the one to many, many, many ... endlessly.

Striking a positive note in the spirit of our wisdom tradition – the reader of this book is encouraged, as a challenge, to embrace the world with all its dangers, uncertainties and ambiguities, to enlarge the scope of personal interests and pursuits, and to ennoble the meaning of success and happiness. The magic of success lies in the ability to transform the entrapping power of the "desire-to-possess" into the unfolding channel of the "desire-to-share."

Happiness Unlimited: Self-Unfoldment is an Interactive World shows the way to convert weaknesses into strengths, traps into transcendence, dreams into accomplishments, and individual desires into Nature's purpose and God's will.

The book provides a manual for global achievers who want to make a qualitative difference to the world in which they live and work – those who want ever-expanding success and whose successes the world and gods celebrate.

Swami Bodhananda

The Sambodh Foundation
New Delhi

ACKNOWLEDGMENTS

In our spiritual tradition, work is considered a labour of love – a devotional offering at the feet of our *Guru* and God. The work on this book is no exception. However, those who are associated with various stages of the production of this book would consider it a privilege and blessing if a few words were said about their contributions.

To a Mumbai audience in November 1998, I delivered these lectures, setting the ball rolling. I thank Mrs. Mridula Bhatnagar, Trustee of Sambodh Foundation, New Delhi, and her sister-in-law, Mrs. Preeti Bhatnagar, of Mumbai, who both worked tirelessly for making this series of talks possible.

Dr. Sangeetha Menon, National Institute of Advanced Studies, Bangalore, as usual took the initiative in preparing the first copy of the manuscript. I warmly acknowledge her effort.

Dr. Ruth Harring, Trustee of The Sambodh Society, Inc., USA, meticulously went through the manuscript with a fine-toothed comb and brought the book to its present level of perfection. Her long hours of labour are evident in every page of the book produced in April 2001 for our western readers and devotees

Finally, I thank Srishti for this new edition for India, retitled and redesigned as *Happiness Unlimited: Self-Unfoldment is an Interactive World*

I offer my gratitude to all those who have in other ways contributed to the work on this book, although their names may not be specifically mentioned here.

Last, but not least, I salute the succession of *Gurus* who out of their motiveless compassion selflessly worked, and are still working, for the creation and preservation of our priceless wisdom tradition, at whose feet this book is a humble offering.

Swami Bodhananda

The Sambodh Foundation
New Delhi
28 August 2002

One

Purity of Mind

ANTAHKARANASUDDHI

It is not the man who has too little,
but the man who craves for more
and more who is poor.
Seneca, Roman Senator

Comfortably Unhappy

The modern individual faces the age-old problem that his ancestors faced – sheer survival – struggling for his or her daily needs of food, shelter and clothing. We struggle and strive. Life is very competitive – so many people chasing so few goods and services in a revolution of rising expectations. Everyone wants the same level of comfort. All of us are struggling, and, at the same time, coming to the realization that mere fulfillment of our material needs is not enough to live a life of quality, a life of total satisfaction. We have arrived at the sad realization that, although we have successfully acquired all the comforts of life, we continue to remain unhappy and discontented.

This is the paradox of modern life – living in luxury, in unprecedented levels of comfort, we are all unhappy! No doubt we have comforts – air-conditioning, medicine and plenty of food. Servants may buzz around us but, in spite of all these comforts, we are unhappy – *comfortably unhappy*.

The mystery is that we are still unable to pinpoint the cause of our own discontent. Why are we unhappy? Ask anyone on the road why he is unhappy! He will answer with a vague gaze, turning the other way. No one will directly say that he or she is unhappy. But we just try to avoid eye contact with our interlocutor. We have no real answer. We cannot say that we are unhappy, but we know that we are unhappy.

This is the ultimate paradox of man – his unhappiness in the midst of comfort. It is this dilemma that we will discuss in this book. It is not that I am going to give you an ultimate solution. We have to find the solution all by ourselves, within our very selves. But, with the help of the *Bhagavad Gita*, we will try together to unravel the problem so that, at the end of reading this book, you will have an idea of the art of right living and be capable of tapping into the highest level of satisfaction. Then, in the evening of your life you will be able to say that you have lived life fully, and you can thank God for all that He has given.

Is this possible? Or are we condemned to live this wretched, dissatisfied life? Some people say that we are condemned to live the way we are living, that we have no escape. We breathe, eat and sleep. We reproduce, become old and then one day we die. The prospect of human life is just that! But our whole being rebels against such a contention. We feel that there is something deeper, there is something profound and sacred, though we know not where to search. Is it a place, a state of mind? Perhaps it is a paradise where we may have every indulgence! What it is, we are not sure. We are unable to express it, like a baby, who is only able to cry and cannot yet utter the words, "I am hungry," or exclaim, "That ant bit me," or proclaim, "I want to sleep!" Similarly, we are all *spiritual* babies. We cry; but we know not what for! We only have a vague sense of an inexpressible need in mind. Is there such a thing as continuous fulfillment? If once we were to achieve such a state, then perhaps we would become quiet and happy.

When the mind becomes serene, satiated and creative, we work unforced, unconditioned by any deficiency needs born of biological and psychological conditioning. The mind will unfold its potential in that state of fullness, convert prior conditioning into an instrument of opportunity.

Continuous Happiness

We have a vague notion about *samadhi* – enlightenment. We know, generally, that the present life is not the life we want to live. How do we reach that state of total satisfaction, where we can say with self-assurance, "*Anando'ham*" – "I am a happy person"? Until today, our idea of happiness was the result of association with desirable objects, our indulgence in personal desires. Our concept of happiness is nothing more than what we gain through indulgence. Hence, we declare, "When I eat chocolates, I am happy." Is it possible to continuously eat chocolates and thus remain in a continuous state of happiness? Unfortunately we cannot increase our happiness by eating more chocolates, although you may want to remain in that state of happiness forever. We want the kind of happiness that is continuous and stable, happiness that we have no fear of losing.

All of us agree, then, that what we ultimately seek is a permanent state of happiness. In fact, the *Upanishads* say, in so many words, "God is happiness." I hope that no one objects to this statement. If I tell you to seek Krishna, you reply, "No, I would rather seek Rama." If I say, "Seek Rama," you respond, "No, I want to seek Jesus Christ." If I advise, "Seek Jesus Christ," you retort, "No, I want the emptiness of a Buddha." If I say, "Okay, then seek emptiness," you suddenly feel puzzled. Such words are merely abstractions. But if I ask you to seek Happiness, then you have no complaint. Happiness is something we understand. We may find the meaning of abstract words in a dictionary, but are we able to have the experience of what those words indicate?

What we want is a continuous experience by which we feel whole and complete, where there is no ripple of desire in our mind, where we function spontaneously, act out of transparent motives. Isn't it that creative, happy, complete state of mind that we all seek, in spite of our inability to articulate it? The only remaining question is, how do we go about it? Until we gain that state of mind we will remain unsatisfied and unhappy persons. So, let us see how we go about this task.

According to the *Bhagavad Gita* and the *Upanishads*, God is Happiness – *Anando brahmeti vyajanat*. "Understand that *Brahman* is Happiness." The word "*Brahman*" is an abstraction, an indicative word. Happiness is something that we all understand; it is not an abstraction. Happiness is something deeply rooted in experience. We *know* what it is. Fortunately, I don't have to describe it to you! Nor do I have to draw a picture of happiness, nor give you a chart of happiness, nor a formula for happiness, nor a happiness tablet! "Happiness" is an experience very deeply embedded in our consciousness. We simply experience it. Just as no one has to teach us how to be hungry – although nowadays that may also be necessary! We have forgotten how to be hungry. Let us explore this analogy further.

Most of our hunger is psychological. Often hunger is only a thought. We think, "It is one o'clock. I must be hungry." Moreover, we continue to feel hungry even after having a sumptuous meal. The fact that food can no longer give us satiation merely indicates our *psychological* hunger. We have lost the capacity to really feel hungry. Many of our diseases are due to our having lost touch with our hunger. We don't enjoy our food. Eating has become a habit, a routine. We always find something wrong with our food and ascribe the reason to the woman of the house. What is not good is in our mental attitude, our mind. Analyze that! If we really feel hunger, if we really taste food, only then are we able to understand the ecstasy of satisfaction.

The satiation we get after eating is something very deep, something experiential; no one needs to teach us that. Satisfaction is a very profound experience. When we are satisfied we may also understand what happiness is.

From the experience of appeasing our hunger we can extrapolate and understand the deep satisfaction that our *soul* seeks. The hunger of your soul! Haven't you felt it? If you have not felt the hunger of the soul, if you have only known pseudo-hunger, then you will not be able to know the meaning of *true* happiness.

The Experience of Happiness

Happiness is something central to our experience. We may, however, be unable to verbalize the experience. The *Upanishads* state that a person who has really touched that Supreme level of satisfaction becomes *muka*, speechless. Is it not true? Whenever there is *real* satisfaction, don't we become speechless? When you first saw the Taj Mahal on a moonlit night – the wonderful 'marble poem' on the banks of Yamuna, shining under the silvery moon – you simply lost your breath, gasped and just stood still without the words to express your wonder. If the Taj Mahal is capable of making you speechless in a state of incomparable ecstasy, what then to say about the experience of Self-unfoldment!

We become silent when the true meaning of happiness is understood: Those who *know* do not speak, and those who speak, do not know. Therefore, if anyone becomes talkative about such a profound experience, know that that person does not *know*. The person who has profound knowledge just remains quiet. Since his heart is full, he becomes silent. Since he knows, he doesn't speak.

Friends, what I write here is *not* an abstraction, not an idea, not even an ideal! You can experience deep happiness and understand it nonverbally. Don't insist that, "Since I don't understand Sanskrit, I'm unable to have this profound experience of Self-unfoldment." Self-unfoldment is something non-verbal. There is no need for you to articulate either the experience or verbalize its expression in life. When the mind is quiet, serene and deep, this experience will overwhelm you. And once this experience takes possession of you, your life becomes a continuous expression of ecstasy. It is *that* creative ecstasy that we are all seeking, that which we cannot obtain from indulgence in desires.

The God whom we seek is Infinite Happiness. That Infinite Happiness is nonverbal. It is not an idea to be grasped intellectually. It is something like the experience of appeasing one's hunger. Once you experience it, even if the whole world contradicts you, you remain unaffected.

Distinguishing Happiness from Pleasure

Compare the experience described above with your ordinary

experience. We think that our happiness comes from indulging in desires. When we indulge in a desire we gain a kind of minimal happiness which we call pleasure. In Vedanta we use the more exacting term, *bhogasukha* – contingent pleasure. We do experience a certain joy when we eat chocolates, see movies or gossip over the phone. That joy is called *bhogasukha*. A *bhogi* ultimately becomes a *rogi* – a sick person. He invariably lands in the hospital, sooner rather than later, with either heart failure, or with a kidney or stomach problem. Every one of his organs becomes dysfunctional. The only remaining functional organ is his brain – because he hardly uses it!

The more we live a physically indulgent life, the more our core withers because we lose touch with and fail to draw from our inner core. The more our inner core dries up, the more we lose our soul, the sacred space within. We become extroverted, material zombies without a spiritual centre. Our existence becomes totally externalized. When we seek temporary happiness in life, our spiritual centre is ignored. An indulgent life gives only transient pleasure and not lasting happiness.

All pleasures finally lead to pain:

> *Ye hi samsparsa-ja bhoga duhkha-yonaya eva te*
> *ady-antavantah, Kaunteya, na tesu ramate budhah*

"Any pleasure is conditioned by time, place, quality of the object, one's state of mind and level of intellect." (Gita *V:22*). Pleasures cannot be lasting. The person whom you loved so much the previous day might become your worst enemy today.

According to the *Bhagavad Gita*, pleasure is only sugar-coated pain. I am not saying that pleasure is unnecessary. Nor am I saying that we should turn totally away from the world with its pleasures and go to the Himalayas and sit in a cave. That is not the purpose of this dialogue. Rather, our purpose is to understand the limitations of pleasure. Pleasures are meaningful in certain contexts but cannot give us lasting satisfaction.

We have to distinguish between these two concepts – the temporary pleasure that we get in desire fulfillment and the *true* happiness that we get in desire-transcendence. The *Gita* states that true happiness cannot come from indulging in desires. In fact, true happiness is attained when desires come to an end and the mind becomes quiet, detached and serene, self-abiding. True happiness is experienced when the mind observes the world in a detached manner. True happiness comes when we enjoy non-judgmental observation tempered by the understanding that pleasure cannot give us the lasting joy we seek. When we relate to our environment with that understanding, then our minds become serene and quiet.

Please understand, I am not advocating that we refrain from relationship with the world. Nor am I saying that we should not enjoy the world. What I am saying is that you should relate to the world, but do so with a mind chastened by the understanding that all pleasures are limited. Pleasures will come and go leading the ignorant to the pit of pain. If you interact with the world with that understanding, your mind remains undisturbed. In that poised mind the ultimate happens – the visitation of the Divine. The experience is indescribable. *Rishis*, the sages who have contemplated this Truth, say that when the mind is serene and quiet, when we see without judging, needing nothing, it experiences an inner awakening. Something very deep and self-transforming happens in that mind. Then you may say that you have arrived, that you are truly happy. That experience is of the sacred dimension.

Ever-Lasting Joy

There are two kinds of *sukha* – joy. One is *bhogasukha*, and the other is *yogasukha*. We will first discuss *yogasukha* – the happiness that we gain by freeing ourselves from the pull of objects and desire. What we seek is spontaneous, natural happiness. Out of that spontaneous happiness arises a very creative person. It is not that after gaining that happiness one sleeps all the time; those whose happiness is spontaneous and natural become very creative and active. Everyone ought to strive for creative happiness and intelligence. That is our goal, our destiny and birthright – to understand and to realize our own inner spiritual joy and fulfillment! Thereafter our perception of deficiency ceases. Gone is the nagging sense of inadequacy. We feel complete and whole.

A *sannyasi* is called "His Holiness" because his happiness is whole – and wholesome. His happiness ceases to depend upon anything. This independent happiness is called *moksa* or *yogasukha* – transcendental bliss. What is meant by *moksa*? By *moksa* we do not mean liberation from the body. Nor do we mean liberation from our family! Sometimes people approach swamis and emphatically announce, "I want to become a *sannyasi*!" If we persistently ask such a person the reason behind his wanting to become a *sannyasi*, he replies, "I had a quarrel with my wife; I'm ready to renounce the world!" That is an insufficient reason to renounce the world and become a *sannyasi*. When there are quarrels that we cannot resolve, when we are exhausted by this interactive world, only then do we think of *sannyasa*! We purchase a train ticket and leave home! But how long will we stay in the *ashram*? After two weeks we start posting letters, requesting our family not to worry and expressing our intention to return soon. Mind is indeed fickle – it always sees the other side as greener!

True *sannyasa* is neither escaping from nor complaining about one's environment and its challenges. True *sannyasa* is renouncing the search for happiness in the world. When you no more seek happiness in relationships or in possessions – that is *sannyasa*. Alas, we seek happiness in relationships, in the office, even in the Lions Club! Why do we join the local Lions Club? To seek happiness? We go because no one at home or at work calls us "lion." In the Lions Club everyone greets each other as "Lion," knowing full well that no one is really a lion, or even faintly has the qualities of the king of beasts. We know we are only rats participating in a "rat race." The pity is that even if we win the rat race, we continue to be rats! We never even become cats, let alone lions!

Relationships cannot give us the true happiness we are seeking. Nor should we expect a relationship to be a source of true happiness. Whereas, if we relate to one another as happy persons, neither situations, nor relationships nor people can make us unhappy. Once we renounce our search for happiness, we come upon the true source of happiness and become a *sannyasi*. Usually, giving up the search for happiness is accompanied by declarations like: "There is absolutely no happiness in this world!" Like the proverbial jackal that philosophized "grapes are sour!", we pronounce the grapes "sour" only because, like the fox, we failed to reach them.

There are some people who renounce the world thinking that there is no happiness to be found. Afterwards, they lead the rest of their lives as miserable, wretched, deprived, suppressed, cynical people. By *sannyasa* we do not mean that kind of an unproductive life. By *sannyasa* we mean the kind of attitude of giving happiness instead of seeking happiness. The more happiness we give, the more happiness blesses us. Like a spring, the more one draws from its waters, the more it gives. By *sannyasa* we mean that kind of happiness. Let us call it "unconditioned happiness." Some people call it unconditional love. When we are happy, we love everyone. When we are unhappy, we have no love for anyone. In the state of unconditional happiness, which is natural and spontaneous, we are One with the entire Universe. We become very creative. This state is called *moksa* or *samadhi*. This is the state we all seek.

Moksa is *mohakshaya* – the ending of delusion. In this non-delusional, natural and creative happiness *all seeking ends*. A person who is happy is a god upon earth. He draws the godly dimension unto himself. To him life is a play, a joyous experience. How does one gain that state of supreme felicity? Arjuna asked the same question of Lord Krishna:

"How do I reach the state of natural happiness leading to timeless spaciousness, empathetically embracing the world?"

Hurdles in Meditation

The answer sometimes given to such an earnest inquiry, is to meditate upon the Spirit, to reflect and detach. But how will we gain that quality of meditation on the Spirit? How will we know where Spirit is? How will we become detached? The more we try to detach the more obsessed we become with the object of our desires. Have you ever confronted that problem? In the seat of meditation, instead of meditating on the true Light, you are upset about your enemy, about those who forgot your birthday, those who have not sent you flowers, or who have not reciprocated your courtesies. During meditation the mind wanders.

Meditation appears to be a very difficult project. We are neither able to meditate, nor are we able to detach. Take this case: Your *guru* had asked you to observe fasting on *ekadasi*, for one day spend your time contemplating *ekam* – the One – instead of the multitude of distractions that dance around you. You were confident that you would be able to give up food, but as the day for fasting approaches, you become panicky. You worry that you will miss morning tea, or breakfast, that sumptuous lunch, and the evening tea! Ironically, on the day of *ekadasi* you end up thinking more about food than God! That from which you have abstained now becomes an obsession for you. Instead of fasting, you feast.

Therefore, you conclude that meditation and detachment are not for people of the world. Your mind is agitated. Desires torment you. Failure in meditation affects your self-esteem. Problems spread their fangs. You feel stressed, tired and fatigued. Meditation seems to be very difficult. Detachment seems to be even more difficult. To draw upon your inner joy seems to be impossible! Your *guru* might recommend that you chant a *mantra*. But after sometime your chanting becomes mechanical and boring. Why are we unable to do all these, though we make every attempt to fast, meditate and detach?

Allow me to tell you the story of a person whose *guru* gave him a *mantra*. This person was very distracted and disturbed, but he wanted peace of mind. So he went to his *guru* and asked him for a technique that would give him peace of mind. The *guru* gave a *mantra* and instructed that he should chant it alone in his *puja* room, keeping it a secret in his own heart. Starting the following day onwards, at four o'clock in the morning, the man began chanting the mantra while alone in his *puja* room. After a few days his wife became suspicious about what he was doing behind the closed doors so early in the morning. It had never been his habit to get up at four o'clock in the morning, take a bath, enter the *puja* room – a place he had never before gone in his entire life – and sit in *padmasana* chanting the *mantra* which his *guru* had given to him. His wife ignored him for the first few days thinking that it would be only another fad and he would easily get over it. But he continued the practice even after three days. On the fifth day, his wife became very anxious and went in the *puja* room and shook him. He opened his eyes. She inquired, "What are you doing?" He replied, "I am meditating and chanting a *mantra* for peace of mind. Can't you see?" His wife insisted, "I also need peace of mind!" Her mind, in fact was in pieces! She requested him to reveal the *mantra* to her as well. He firmly obeyed his *guru's* instructions and refused to reveal the *mantra* to her. Finally, she issued an ultimatum – "Either me or your *mantra*!" The man became utterly confused and bewildered! While he was pondering what he should do, given this unexpected dilemma, his wife became so furious that she collected all her belongings, hailed a taxi and drove away. Before the poor man realized what had happened, everything had happened! He arrived on his front doorstep only to see the taxi disappearing. Dropping onto a chair in utter despair, he heaved a sigh. But then, in the quietude of his wife's absence, another thought rippled in his mind, and he chuckled, "The *mantra* worked!" But did the *mantra* work? Alas, no! After reaching her ancestral home, his wife phoned him and recanted, "Pick me up as soon as your meditation is over."

We learn from such a story that employing tricks and techniques, with the expectation of attaining happiness, simply does not work. Unless we understand the import of what we are seeking, we will not be able to have lasting joy. How to gain lasting happiness? A *mantra* does not work because, with an agitated mind, we are incapable of fully concentrating. Our minds labour under a million and one pressures and desires. Such a mind only reacts – all the time. A mind that helplessly reacts cannot meditate. It is not under control. It springs into reaction. Without reason anger is aroused. How can such a mind – one that continuously reacts with anger, with jealousy, with greed, or with lust – meditate?

Anger, jealousy, greed, judgment, comparison, etc., are inhibitory factors. They prevent us from discovering and unfolding our inner potential. We do more harm to ourselves when we become angry. We do more harm to ourselves when we are jealous. Our reactions spew poison all around us.

It is not the object of our anger or jealousy that suffers, but the *subjective you*. Reactions cause unhappiness. For instance, we leave the hall after a *Gita* lecture with a serene mind, but if we don't find our shoes, which we had left outside the hall, we immediately react: "See the effect of the *kaliyuga*; someone has stolen my shoes!" The shoes might be lying there; someone might have just kicked them aside a little, but we react instantly! When we are angry we even call our own child "the son of a donkey." And, before we are able to correct ourselves, the child retorts, "Dad, this is the only truth you have ever spoken!" It is at that moment that we realize what we so foolishly uttered. But now we have said it, and we cannot take our statement back. It has become part of the cosmic record. It booms and echoes and re-echoes in cosmic space and eventually makes us feel like a real donkey!

Unless we have a firm grip, unless we are able to apply the brakes and control our reactions, we will not be able to meditate. But, we shouldn't expect to erase our reactions overnight. What we need is objectivity and balance that enable us to avoid unnecessary reactions. It is not that we are happy with our reactions. After every reaction, don't we feel wretched and regretful?

What is Reaction?

Reaction is a response over which we have little or no control and about which we later feel guilty. Once the consequences of a reaction descend upon us, we have second thoughts. The consequences are unpalatable. When we react, we fail to think. We think of the consequences of our behavior only *after* reacting. Then we feel ashamed and remorseful, "I should not have reacted the way I did." The dictum is: look before you leap.

Reactions pour out from us like white ants from rotten wood. Due to our reactions we fail to focus either upon our work or upon our values – so much less upon our own spiritual, sacred space. Due to reactions, our attention on work falters. Unable to centre spiritually we fail to live up to our values.

Deprived of all these abilities, we become confused and bewildered, a state that Arjuna experienced as, *Karpanya-dos'opahata-svabhavah prcchami tvam dharma-sammudha-cetah* – "Bhagavan, I have been living like a *kripana*, a wretch; I am unable to use my faculties properly" (*Gita* II:7). Such people float about like wooden logs in a river. Like dry leaves, they are tossed about in the stormy passions of the mind.

Uncontrolled emotions and drives create havoc in life. How to take charge of our life so that when situations arise we make the right choices, *respond* rather than *react*? When I say that we must control our reactions, I don't mean that we should become stone-like. For instance, if someone stamps on your toes with his heavy boot, crushing your toenails and flesh under his shoe, you need not keep a stony silence. That would be foolish. You can, of course, politely ask the person to remove his boot from your toe. But then, don't impulsively punch his nose! He might be a local police inspector and drag you to the police station ...!

Responding in the Right Measure

We should be wise enough to evaluate situations and invoke the right response commensurate to each situation. The *right* response in the *right* measure – that is wisdom, that is clarity. We don't have to sit like a stone, nor do we have to react like a headless chicken. We can choose to be a very mindful person. We should know what we want and how to go about achieving our goals. We should be free to make the right choice, to respond appropriately. The ability to choose our responses is called *response-ability*. How do we gain such power over ourselves? It is very important that, as spiritual seekers, we have certain control over our reactions. Reactions are called *mala* – impurity. Impurities are the inhibiting factors that disturb both our meditation and our relationships in and with the world.

Our operative mind, *antahkarana*, is the instrument of response. We know that when sensations flow into our mind through the sense organs, the mind processes that information and impulsively reacts – sometimes violently, sometimes uncontrollably – with Pavlovian-like responses! We respond to situations through the organs of action. How do we manage this traffic of life, the receiving of stimuli and responding to stimuli? Do we have both red and green lights? If you have no system of traffic lights, then nothing moves smoothly.

The ability to choose our responses to situations is an important asset in our spiritual progress. Without that ability we are unable to reach our intended spiritual destination. We will be caught up in a traffic jam. You might say, "I don't care. I will chant my *mantra* and do my *puja*!" But, this way, you will never reach your destination. How do we remove the impurities of our mind gathered over long periods of unconscious living? When we look at the sky, what we see now is only a haze. Will the clouds of our mind ever clear away so that we see the sky, stars and the moon with clarity?

Antahkaranasuddhi and *Sadhana*

The first condition for *antahkaranasuddhi* is awareness of the need for inner purity. *Antahkaranasuddhi* is important in all spiritual pursuits. It is also called as *bhutasuddhi*, *sattvasuddhi*, or *manasuddhi*. *Antahkarana* is the inner equipment. It is comprised of our feelings, thoughts, rational faculties, memories and sense of identity, all together. It is the instrument of both receiving stimuli and responding. How to purify the *antahkarana*? How to make the mind a healthy working-instrument? *Antahkaranasuddhi* is a very important asset in spiritual evolution. We react in terms of anger, jealousy, comparison, judgment, greed and lust. These reactions are both the results as well as further causes of mental impurity.

The second condition for purifying the mind is an active life in this world. Usually, when we think of purifying the mind, we think of leaving for the Himalayas and taking up residence in a cave. Since there isn't anyone to disturb us in the Himalayas, the mind appears to be pure. We assume that inactivity or special spiritual activities will purify the mind naturally – just as if by leaving a dirty well undisturbed, the water will appear to be pure. But throw a stone into the well, and the water becomes muddied. Provocation is a necessary condition for practicing non-reaction, just as mounting and balancing on a horse is a necessary first step in learning horse riding.

Here is a story: Someone went to his *guru* and said, "My well is contaminated and foul smelling because a dog fell in and died." The *guru* gave the man a *mantra*, instructed him to chant it one thousand and eight times along with offering a few pinches of *vibhuti* (sacred ash) and *tulsi* leaves into the well. "Then," the *guru* said, "the water will become pure." After one week the man came back and reported to the *guru* that, although he chanted the *mantra*, the foul smell only worsened. Now he couldn't even go near the well. Then the *guru* asked, "What did you do?" The man replied, "I have put the *vibhuti* and *tulsi* leaves into the well, as you instructed, and chanted the *mantra* too." "Did you remove the dead dog?" And the man shrieked, "But you didn't tell me to remove the dead dog!" You may chant the *mantra* but unless you remove the dead dog – i.e., unless the mind learns to avoid reactions and to choose appropriate responses – you will not be able to attain the proper result.

Now, two questions remain: How do we learn to choose our responses, and, how can we apply the brakes to our mind? These questions introduce the third condition for *antahkaranasuddhi* – the conscious, deliberate practice of non-reaction in action and in interaction.

There is a discipline for gaining *antahkaranasuddhi*. That discipline is called *sadhana*. *Sadhana* is something that we practice deliberately; it is a deliberate application of values in our daily life. We may be angry, but we can also choose *not* to be angry. The practice of certain values is to become our *sadhana*, to be practiced in our daily living. For *antahkaranasuddhi* the most important condition is that we should remain in the business of the world. Being in the world and interacting with the world are both necessary conditions for *antahkaranasuddhi*. The *suddhi*, purity, we gain in the Himalayas is only partial and superficial. There you might behave like a saint, but only because your detractors are not there to disturb you! When you come back to your home and to society, you become the same old person. The impurities are within us, not due to outside causes. Therefore, one should *not* avoid the world of relationships. Relationships provoke us. Relationship means constant provocation. Provocation reveals our impurities. We have expectations of others. Others also have expectations of us. As we provoke one another in relationships we also have the opportunity to apply discipline and to transform provoking situations and invoke opportunities.

It is only when we mount a horse and ride it that we can apply the reins and bring the horse under our control. There is little meaning in saying that we will control a horse without mounting him! We must be in relationship to purify the mind. We acquired impurities through relationship. The same relationship is to be used to liquidate impurities. Hence, be in relationship – and *then* apply the values, "I will not react. I will not be judgmental. In anger, I will watch. I know the debilitating effect of anger on me that prevents me from unfolding my full potential." To the enterprising individual, all obstacles are opportunities!

An angry person cannot inspire others. Even those who serve us will be de-motivated by violent outbursts. If in anger you ask someone to bring a hot cup of tea, he will bring you a cup of cold coffee! You don't inspire him. To get work done through others, we should be quietly persuasive. To bring out your full potential *and* the potential of others, we should learn the art of appropriate response.

Be in the Midst of the World

Values like humility, non-violence, simplicity, sharing, etc., (*Gita* XIII:7-11), ought to be applied *while* engaged in relationships. Then, over a period of time, we will be able to master the mind. We will be able to lead a harmonious and poised life. We will be able to engage in an interactive life without getting upset or hurt, without the feeling of rejection. When we attain such a state of mind, the Lord assures us that we will be ready for meditation. This state is called *samatvam – samatvam yoga ucyate* – "balance of mind" (II:48). Ride the horse of life. While riding you may fall off, but that is the only way to learn. When you are atop the horse, rock with the rhythm of the horse. As we move forward in life, we will learn to balance the mind.

Antahkaranasuddhi is to be practiced in the midst of relationships, by applying certain values. These values are not for the world but for *you*! When you refrain from anger, you are the beneficiary. Of course, the other person is benefited to an extent, but the main beneficiary is you, yourself. When you are not jealous it is not the other person who is benefited. You master the galloping mind.

In the *Bhagavad Gita*, Lord Krishna says, *Aruruksor muner yogam karma karanam ucyate* – "If you want to attain the state of yoga, of balancing the mind in relationships and interactions, you have to involve in activity" (*Gita* VI:3). Gradually, you will be able to control and balance the mind. *Yog'arudhasya tasy'aiva samah karanam ucyate.* "One who has attained a balanced mind, practices meditation as a means of Self-unfoldment" (*Gita* VI:3).

Values are to be practiced while we interact with the world. It is also said, *Yajna-dana-tapah-karma na tyajyam iti c'apare.* "Neither renounce *yajna, dana* nor *tapa karma*" (*Gita* XVIII:3). The ability to work as a team (*yajna karma*), the willingness to share (*dana karma*), and the resolve to live on limited resources (*tapa karma*) are important spiritual values to be cultivated. You should be able to live a simple, sharing life, a life where you work collectively to realize progressively higher objectives without any interpersonal problems. Over a period of time this ability to live and work in the world without getting hurt and agitated will be gained.

The resulting dynamic and quiet mind is a precondition for fruitful meditation. The meditation-worthiness of your mind is gauged by your ability to concentrate on chosen work, by your ability to balance the mind in gain and loss, and by your unshaken endeavour to understand the Truth. Now, let us assume that you have a certain degree of inner purity and concentration. The next question is how do you come to *know* the Truth? How do you feel the Truth? How do you remain steadfast in the Truth?

First we need to understand the value of *antahkaranasuddhi* and put its principles into practice. A person whose mind is pure has the opportunity to receive *higher* Truth.

Two

Ways of Knowing

PRAMANA

In science, absence of proof
is not proof of absence.
Scientist

The Ultimate Goal

The ultimate goal of humankind is to experience unconditional happiness, a happiness that does not change but is always new and is not born of indulgence. Anything born of indulgence is perishable. Because of the changing nature of the material world, the happiness that is gained from contact with material objects also has to change – whereas the happiness that we are talking about is imperishable. In Sanskrit the word used for happiness is *sukham*. *Sukham* means "spaciousness." Unconditional happiness is the experience of spaciousness, accommodation. You cease to be in conflict with anyone or anything. Suppose someone wants to sit in your chair. Either he has to push you out or you have to voluntarily vacate. There cannot be space for both of you in a limited space. When you lack space, you are in conflict. By contrast, the happiness being discussed here is *pure* spaciousness. There is abundant space within and around you. You can accommodate anyone. Conflict ceases. With freedom from conflict, we live in harmony with existence. Hence, this state – which is wholeness – is also called *holiness*.

We all want total fulfillment in which we are naturally and spontaneously happy. I have no doubt that all of us will be aspiring for that state, if not today then tomorrow. If this is our objective in life then we cannot afford to live in ignorance, or ignoring that state. Neither can we postpone our efforts to gain that fullness. Postponement only brings conflict, unhappiness and misery. There is real urgency as far as this pursuit is concerned.

Have you ever met anyone happy with his unhappiness? Can you be happy with unhappiness? Impossible! Therefore, we must strive to gain that state, if not in this life then in the next. We are choiceless regarding this matter! As Indians we have the additional consolation of a next life, nevertheless strive we must.

Happiness is not mere pleasure. It is a state of spaciousness, an all-accommodating state of Consciousness. It is called *braahmi stitih* – abiding in *Brahman*. The *Gita* says, *Esa braahmi sthitih Partha n'ainam prapya vimuhyati* – "This is the state of abidance in *Brahman*, O Arjuna, where there is no delusion, no further seeking" (II:72). Seeking comes to an end; there is no further need to seek happiness. Instead you go around giving, sharing your joy and bliss, since you have an overabundance. You are rich, wealthy, a *Maharaj*. You can share your joy that is available freely. Life expresses as a continuous thanksgiving.

Self-abidance is total health. You feel a sense of wellness, an incredible lightness about you, joyousness. Being joyous, your energy overflows and creativity abounds. This is not a passive state of inactivity. It is a very dynamic state of continuous activity. Whatever you do, you do to the best of your ability. If you are a poet, you are an excellent poet. If you are an artist, your art will flourish. If you are a housewife, you will be an accomplished housewife. Even if you are a scavenger, you will be an efficient scavenger!

Don't be afraid that this experience will make you like a stone. No, it is extreme creativity. If you are not creative and still say, "I have realized," that is a lie. You cannot be non-creative and realized. A realized person is an accomplished person; one who is awakened to his full potential has to be a creative person. Whatever he does, he does to perfection.

Lord Krishna says in the *Bhagavad Gita*,

> *Na me Partha'sti kartavyam trisu lokesu kimcana*
> *nanavaptam avaptavyam varta eva ca karmani*

"I have nothing to gain nor lose in this world. Still, I am very active" (III:22). When the mind is free from conflict and desire, then it opens to creativity. You must have observed this happening. Whenever the mind was creative, it was free from desire. For example, while writing an examination, if you don't worry about the final result then you will be able to bring out your full potential, because thoughts don't interfere with your work. Whenever you have been highly creative, your mind has been absolutely free from thought. It enjoys total alertness, total concentration without distraction. So let us not imagine that a person who has awakened to that state, who is totally happy, will become an inactive person. He will live life to its fullness. Whatever his field, he will be a highly accomplished person. This is what we want and this is our destiny. Nobody can snatch it or hide it from us. Our destiny is to live our life in its fullness, be constantly happy and joyous, and make life a celebration.

People sometimes request that I read their hands and predict their destinies. It is unnecessary to read the hand to predict your destiny. Your destiny is your infinity; you have infinite power within you. Discover it. Tap it. Access it and make your life an enjoyable experience.

To realize God, to live in God Consciousness, to be self-realized, are all different expressions of the same goal – which is to go beyond all contradictions and conflicts. Patanjali calls it *samadhi*. Vedanta calls it *moksa*. To a *bhakta* it is *sayujya* – to interact with the Lord as Hanumanji interacted with Rama, or to dance with Krishna as Radha.

Whichever expression you use to describe it, whichever religion you belong to, your goal is the same. We all want enlightenment. Hold this in your mind. Let this be inscribed in your mind, so that when you move in this charming world, you remember your goal and will not falter in your striving. The world may label you as useless. Your children may ignore you. Your friends may abandon you when you are of no more use to them. One day you may be thrown out from work. Your own body will start troubling you and death will approach like an old devouring python. As everything collapses around you, this goal becomes your only anchor in life.

Purity of Mind: *Antahkaranasuddhi*

Having understood that the goal of life is to gain fullness, what one needs next is inner purity. The mind is the vehicle through which you enter into the world of *samsara*. By the same vehicle you can exit from the world of misery and enter into the world of *sayujya* or *nirvana*. The vehicle is the same for both exit and entry. For instance, imagine what might happen if you buy a motorbike for your teenage son. One possibility is that he can drive that motorbike recklessly and fall into a nearby ditch. However, that same bike can carry him to the college where he can further his studies. With the same instrument, the same vehicle, we can ride to the land of doom or to the land of dreams, opportunities and blessings. Both possibilities exist.

Mind is the cause of bondage as well as liberation – *mana eva manusyanam karanam bandhamoksayoh*. No animal has a mind. Neither do trees or stones have minds – at least not the mind as we understand it. Furthermore, without a mind they all seem to be happy. Have we ever seen an unhappy banyan tree or an unhappy buffalo? Have you ever seen two buffaloes discussing their miseries and sorrows, or their philosophies? Impossible! Only man – the roof and crown of creation – is unhappy, and that is because he has a mind. A discerning mind prods you to your full potential, bids you to go *beyond* the body, beyond its own limitations, *beyond* contradictions and pairs of opposites. The mind intimates higher possibilities for you. But today, the materialistic mind is thinking only of acquiring, aggrandizing and indulging beyond its need.

No doubt we have certain needs. When we are thirsty, we need water. Can we claim we are *mahapurusa mahatma* and hence don't need water? When we are hungry, we need food. When we feel cold, we need shelter. When it rains, we need a roof over our head. No doubt, we need all these basic comforts, and all these basic needs can be fulfilled. There is no difficulty. If someone is hungry you can give him food, but how much food can he eat? After eating the maximum he will say, "Enough!" How much water can one drink? How many houses do we need? How many outfits can one wear? Our natural needs can be fulfilled, in fact, must be fulfilled. As Gandhi said, "God has provided for your needs, but not for your greed." Let us not be foolish and ignore our basic needs. We require these needs to be fulfilled, but your greed? We cannot expect our need for security, love or happiness to be fulfilled by material excess. Those needs can only be fulfilled from inside. Even if someone says that he loves you, don't you doubt him? Your doubt is that since you have never loved anyone, how can anyone love you? That is insecurity. Your suspicion is aroused – "This pretender expects something from me!"

No one *gives* you security. No one *gives* you love. No one gives you happiness. You have to discover love, security and happiness within yourself – discover your inner centre, as solid as a rock. Until you discover that inner centre, you will wobble, disturbed and lost in this world.

You need a mind that is relatively pure. As long your mind wanders in this world, attracted to worldly things, correction is required – a reordering of the mind. Movement into the world has been an unconscious habit – you see something interesting, though you know that your happiness is within – and habit carries you away. Mind is to be controlled, purified. Mind is to be moulded into a mature, balanced mind. Purifying of mind is called *antahkaranasuddhi*.

The impurity of mind, *asuddhi*, is reaction. We constantly react even though we know that reaction harms. We know that we should not be angry, we should not be nasty, we should not be jealous or fear anyone. We know better, but we sustain all these habits. We have values, but we have not understood the personal importance of those values. Neither do we command the mind in accordance with those values. We often forget the benefit of living those values. What are the benefits of non-reaction and keeping our mind in balance? By responding, rather than reacting, we gain maturity of mind.

Non-reaction is not opposed to responding. We must respond, but we need not react. With a mature and non-reacting mind, one is capable of understanding spiritual truths. Spiritual enlightenment is possible only in a quiet mind.

The Meaning of *Yoga*

Yoga has three meanings. One is, *yogah karmasu kausalam* – "efficiency and concentration in work" (*Gita* II.50). If you can concentrate fully in your work, whatever the nature of the work, then you can be called a *yogi*. You must be able to concentrate. For example, say that you are at a lecture. You must be able to concentrate on what is being said. Some people find it impossible to concentrate on their present activity or environment. They are "not here," so to speak. They have not left behind extraneous thoughts of home life or some unsettling incident! They are physically present, but mentally absent. After the lecture is over, when they are driving back home, they wonder, "What did he say?" Sometimes they ask for the audiotape of the lecture thinking that they will be able to concentrate later on while listening to the recording. What do you think? Will they be better able to concentrate? Not at all! When you are at a lecture, you are supposed to concentrate – which you don't do. When you drive home, you are supposed to concentrate on the driving – which you don't do. This only creates problems for yourself and others.

The first meaning of *yoga* is the ability to concentrate.

Another meaning of *yoga* is, *samatvam yoga ucyate* – "balance of mind" (*Gita* II.48). A detached state of mind is called *yoga*. To gain a balanced state of mind, you have to remain active in this world. Unless you are active and establish relationships, unless you give and take, unless you invest in others and trust them, you cannot gain a balanced mind. Every relationship involves risk *and* opportunity. The energy you invest in any relationship is a risk. Take that risk. Keep your mind in balance. Remain detached, and when your mind is quiet, you will enjoy Self-abidance.

The third meaning of *yoga* is, *samadhav acala buddhih* – "an ability to draw upon your inner resources" (*Gita* II.53). You have infinite resources within, an infinite ability to love, give, share and create. You can even invoke health from within. But, unfortunately, we begin the day by saying, "I don't feel well today; I have a headache." When you say that you have a headache, the whole world will echo – *tathastu* – so be it – amen! When you have a headache people are happy – they can exploit you. Therefore, don't accept such autosuggestion. Don't acquiesce to the thought, "I am miserable."

Yoga is the ability to draw from your own inner resources. The *Gita* says, *Samadhav acala buddhih tada yogam avapsyasi* – "When your mind is abiding in *samadhi*, when you are able to draw from that source, then you are in *yoga*" (II:53). *Samadhi* is the *atman*, the source of infinite potentiality, the field of infinitude.

These different meanings of *yoga* are relevant to our pursuit of the Spirit: 1) *Yoga* is the ability to concentrate; 2) *Yoga* is the ability to balance your mind; 3) *Yoga* is also the ability to draw from our inner resources. I call these *yogas* "three levels of intelligence" – the IQ, EQ and SQ – intelligence quotient, emotional quotient and spiritual quotient. These three ideas are important for your spiritual well-being: to discover your infinitude from within yourself; to maintain a balanced mind; and to avoid violent reaction.

A spiritual person is not a recluse. A recluse is a neurotic person afraid of the world. One doesn't become a spiritual person by being afraid of the world. Arjuna wanted to run away from the battlefield. He said to Krishna that he did not know what to do. He did not want to kill his kith and kin. He pleaded with Lord Krishna to allow him to retire to the forest and do *Krishnajapa* and meditation. Arjuna thought Krishna would be pleased and humoured by this request, but Krishna instructed Arjuna to stay put and fight the battle.

The only way to discover who you are is to clean up the mess you have created in your conscious mind – the unconscious continuum. There is no way to spiritual progress other than active engagement with the world. You *cannot* run away. Where will you run? Wherever you are, you will have carried along your problematic mind. Therefore, it is better that you stay wherever you are and work out your inner complexes. It is an inner process.

Interactions are important. Give and take is important. But don't expect what you give to come back from the same source. You need a subtle intellect to understand that what you give returns to you a thousand-fold, but perhaps not directly from the recipient of your favour. But where is the patience to think on these lines!

Don't cut off your relationships in the name of spirituality. In fact spirituality is embracing the whole world, expanding your network of relationships, not only with human beings, but also with animals, trees and the entire environment. Modern ecological principles give us an idea of the importance of cooperation and coexistence among all life forms.

Means of Knowing

Keep these ideas clearly in mind as we go on to discuss, *pramana*, the means of knowing. When we talk about happiness or God or spirituality, we must know the meaning of these terms. Knowledge is very important. I must know what is happiness, *feel* my happiness, and *be* happiness in order to know what is God. I must feel God within me, not as an abstract, theological concept. Theologians may write a lot about God, but have they tasted the joy of being with God? See their miserable looks and unhappy, greedy faces. But look at Jesus Christ on the cross. Even when he was hanging from three nails with blood dripping – even in that state of agony – he uttered these magnanimous words, "O God, forgive them; they know not what they do." What is the source of that statement, that *consciousness*? Christ even loved His tormentors, because in the expansive consciousness of Jesus Christ there was no tormentor, no enemy, no friend. He saw everyone as an expression of the same Spirit.

It is a question of knowing, of feeling, very deeply. When you know the Spirit, your hair will literally stand on end. When a devotee hears about Krishna, he feels ecstatic, a current passing through his body. But when you and I hear about Krishna, nothing happens. We might just as well look around and think about Krishnan Nair or Krishnaswami who were good athletes in earlier days.

Not only should you know happiness, you should feel it and be it. Feelings are fleeting, therefore, mere feeling is not enough. Mere knowing is also not enough. One must move into it, one must become one with it, like a river becoming one with the ocean after which it cannot separate from the ocean. We are seeking that kind of experience. First let us understand what is knowledge and means of knowing. Then gain and experience that knowledge.

The Limitations of Science

Unfortunately, in the modern world, all our knowledge is head-oriented – logical, sensate, theoretical, objective and impersonal. It does not create any feeling in us. In his effort to control nature and create objects of pleasure, the modern man has come to a stage where he resides in the head region – like Descartes statement, "I think therefore I am." Modern man has no heart. He has no being, no feelings. Abilities to feel and to empathize have disappeared. We have become like computers. Although modern science, with the help of technology, has created an atmosphere of abundance around us it has spoiled our sensitivities. We have lost our souls, our feelings and moral sensitivity. We are over-critical and have become cynics.

At the same time we are gradually realizing that the scientific method of knowing is not the "be all and end all" of knowing. Today, science admits its limitations. It verged on Vedantic awareness when it finally conceded that matter is only a range of probabilities. Physicists have become interested in meditation and find the words of ancient rishis meaningful. When the rishi said, *Tadejati tannaijati taddure tadvantike* – "It moves and it moves not, it is far and it is near, it is smaller than the smallest and bigger than the biggest" (*Isavasya Upanishad* 5) – science considered this ancient wisdom the mere blabbering of an infantile mind. Today modern physics has come to accept the paradoxical conclusion that matter can appear as either a particle or a wave, and that ultimately there is no such thing as matter. It has also concluded that there is constant change and that there is nothing absolute about experience. Enquiry into consciousness has now become important since consciousness seems to be the stable factor underlying all experience.

Let us, for the moment, abandon science and explore the notion of Consciousness along Vedantic lines. We may doubt our own existence, but it is impossible to conclude that we do *not* exist. If we inquire whether or not we exist, our next question ought to be, "Just who is asking this question?" Aren't you, as a questioner, conscious of your doubt? It follows that our own existence cannot be doubted. We exist as Consciousness. What the rishis of yore saw in their meditation is now talked about in the world of modern science!

The scientific method of enquiry, of cold logic and observation that excludes the observer as a datum, is not comprehensive enough. Through the scientific method we can only see the outer material aspects of our existence that the sense organs (and their technological extensions – the microscope, the telescope, etc.) can reach. But there are limits to what the senses can grasp. Aristotle was the greatest logician of his times, and he held that he would be able to understand the mystery of the universe through logic. The sage, Diogenes, thought of humbling Aristotle. He knew that Aristotle went for an evening walk along the seashore. One day Diogenes went to the seashore and started making little holes on the beach. He took a little water in his hand, brought it back and poured it into the holes. Aristotle saw this and asked him, "What are you doing? Why are you taking water by hand and pouring it into little holes?" Diogenes replied, "I am trying to empty the ocean by shifting the water from the ocean to these little holes I've made on the shore." Aristotle laughed and thundered, "How foolish it is to think that you can ever empty the ocean by this method!" The sage retorted, "You are equally foolish to think that you can solve the mystery of the universe through logic."

Progress and Regress

The kind of knowledge which we acquire through logic is based on our limited exposure and understanding. Logic is totally inadequate in knowing the Spirit and the full potential of the human being. We understand this from our experience. We pride ourselves about the great progress technology has made, exclaiming that everyone now has a television and a car and a washing machine. Our expectation about a national leader is one who can ensure all these comforts for us. But now where are we? In the process of obtaining comforts, we have spoiled the environment! Today, we have neither fresh air to breathe nor clean water to drink. We are condemned to live on an overheating planet.

We have two coordinates, progress on one side and nature on the other. The more we consume – the more we rely upon air-conditioning, the more we drive vehicles – the less healthy we become. We are becoming unhealthy as a result of progress! I am not condemning so-called progress. I am only reflecting upon the limits and limitations of progress. The methodology that science has developed over the last two hundred years is inadequate. It fails to address the problem in totality. Take, for example, the field of medicine. Medical science always looked for particular causes for disease – a germ, bacterium or virus. If you have a headache a tablet is prescribed. The headache then becomes a stomachache. Another tablet is given to cure the stomachache. The stomachache becomes a backache and you are given two more tablets. Now, with the pain in your arm, you suspect a heart attack, for which more tablets are given. Finally, when the medical bill comes, you really have a massive heart attack!

The body has its own intelligence, but we abuse that innate intelligence, and through disuse our whole system becomes disorganized. We have lost our physical intelligence. We don't know how much or when to eat. We forget how to let the body repair itself when it is unwell.

What has happened to the family? What has happened to the traditional support systems of society? In our effort to indulge and pursue narcissistic goals, families are disintegrating. As a result, the whole of society disintegrates. What is there to hold onto? There is no lasting faith – we believe only in what we see. We are in a mess. Technology has done much good, but it has simultaneously failed us. Logic has done humanity good, but it too has failed us. Technology promised us to take to El Dorado, the land of honey and milk. We have been led up the garden path and were left in a ditch! Now, we must use our intelligence to solve the problems that science and technology have created. What do we need? Do we need progress *or* ecological health? Can we afford to choose one over the other? We need both – overall health as well as progress.

The time has come for us to think deeply. We have to consider the future of our children, the future of our country, as well as the future of the planet. We cannot afford to continue a profligate lifestyle. A solution has to be sought.

Knowledge through Sense Perception: *Pratyaksa Pramana*

The means of knowledge where sense organs are used is called *pratyaksa pramana*. You see the world through the five sense organs. You see through the eyes. You hear through the ears. You smell through the nose. You taste through the tongue. You feel the texture of different things and movement of the air with the skin. In this way we gather information through our sense organs. We perceive only a fraction of reality through these avenues of knowledge. At the same time it is essential to employ these faculties to know and relate to the material world. If you need to walk from here to there, eyes and legs are required. Don't try to meditate to reach from here to there! Your sense organs are vital to the functioning and maintenance of your body. You need your sense organs to know the external world, but this *pramana* is inadequate for gaining knowledge of all levels. For example, you cannot use your eyes to hear music. The nature of the object predetermines the *pramana*, the means of knowledge that we employ. Sense organs are limited and can give you only sensate knowledge. But there is much more to know than mere sensory objects.

Let us apply these ideas. For example, what do we generally do to gain happiness? We look to nature, go shopping or interact with objects in our environment. We hear, see, touch, smell and taste and use our sensory contacts to derive happiness. We do get some pleasure by the application of sensory knowledge, but we cannot be really happy. The five sense organs are essential to maintain the body, but you are *not* just the body! Your needs do not end by nourishing the body. In fact all our philosophical problems begin after a nourishing meal. Our politicians like to keep the masses in poverty – because once people have enough to eat they start asking inconvenient questions!

We also have a need for respect, dignity, individuality, love and happiness. We have a need to transcend to higher fields of experience. We can insure our physical preservation through sensate knowledge, but the mind needs nourishment, too. What do you do to nourish the mind?

Knowledge through Inference: *Anumana Pramana*

Another means of knowing is logical activity. In Vedanta it is called *anumana* – inference. You can use logic to see your future. You see connections between causes and effects – that such causes have produced such results. This is inference. We use inference to gain security and to logically understand the world. Through logic we have and can create technology and understand the way the world works.

Data flows through our sense organs. We process the data through logical processes and come to conclusions that help us in choice-making and decision-making. But logic can sometimes lead us to wrong conclusions, and logic doesn't help us to know Truth in its fullness! Logic need not always give us the truth, although its purpose is to arrive at Truth. Through logical thinking we intend to reach Truth and Happiness. But we know that the more analytical we are, the more confused we become. Since for every proposition there is opposition, it is difficult for us to take a decision through analytical thinking. If you say that the world is good, an alternative opinion may hold that the world is bad. Logical analysis cannot take you to a definite conclusion. That is why it is said, "Analysis is paralysis." We all suffer caught in that trap.

The modern world generates a glut of information and, often, contradictory information. So much information floods into our brain that often it creates confusion. That is why sometimes people get fed up with logic and give it up totally. But giving up logic is another extreme.

Logic is often an imperfect instrument for analyzing and processing information. Though logical reasoning is needed to a certain extent, we can't *totally* depend upon it. Even great scientists do not entirely depend upon logic. Whenever there were discoveries, great quantum leaps in science, it was logic that took a back seat. Those discoveries happened as a result of breakthroughs. Our tendency is to think routinely. We discover something new when we break the routine and have discontinuities in our thinking.

Today we have advanced jet fighters that circle the world in two or three hours. When the Wright brothers had proposed to put together a flying machine the US government became concerned. They were worried that the brothers might crash and die. The government instituted a committee of experts, vice chancellors and chief engineers, who studied the proposal for two years and came to the conclusion that a flying machine was impossible. By that time, the Wright brothers had already flown the first flying machine.

Breakthroughs in Understanding

Our mind generally thinks in a routine manner. But sometimes when we give up thinking, after long analysis of a problem, breakthroughs happen. When we go beyond sensate information and logic, insights flash before our mind's eye. Two famous stories, one about Archimedes and another about Newton, suggest something about such breakthroughs. In Archimedes' case, the king wanted him to measure the volume of his gold. How to measure the volume – what today we know as specific gravity – was Archimedes' problem.

Archimedes pondered the problem and was puzzled. "How to do it?" he wondered. The ordinary method was to weigh an object in a balance, but that method could not give him the actual volume. Tired of thinking in the sultry weather of Greece, Archimedes finally gave up and decided to take a refreshing bath. When Archimedes dipped into the bathtub, the water overflowed. Suddenly, it struck him! The specific gravity, the density of an object, is equivalent to the water it displaces! Archimedes ran through the streets of Athens, crying "*Eureka!*" Such was his scientific breakthrough.

The story of Newton is similar. He had been thinking about why things fall. He could not understand, on the other hand, why the stars and the planets move in certain trajectories rather than fall. So, one day he was tired of thinking and happened to sit under an apple tree. Then an apple fell on his nose. Of course it broke his nose bridge. Newton looked at the apple and, rather than eat it, he thought about the incident. From this incident came his wonderful discovery – the theory of gravity. "Everything was hidden in darkness prior to Newton. And then the Lord said, 'Let Newton be,' and everything came to light." With the fall of the apple everything came to light for him. He had a breakthrough in his understanding.

Feeling as Knowing

We have to understand that the sensate method (*pratyaksha pramana*) and the logical method (*anumana pramana*) are not the only ways of knowing. *Feeling* can be another means of understanding. Science does not recognize feeling as a means of knowing. For the scientist, feelings are only the body chemistry. Physical sciences reduce feelings to chemical reactions – whether it is love for your children or love for the country. Feelings, for the physicist, are only the flow of electrons. There is no difference between electricity in an electrical wire and the electricity in your brain. But you know that your love for your child cannot be compared to electricity flowing in an electric wire! Modern science has no way of knowing about your *feelings*. We do have feelings, emotions, a sense of sacredness – a higher level of feeling. How do you calculate the value of an emotion? How do you measure the sacredness of a feeling? There is no scientific test for understanding the value of Truth, the value of love, respect for elders or the feeling of sacredness. How can you prove moral understanding or quantify the value of Truth? Certain other ways of knowing are needed as the famous German philosopher, Immanuel Kant, indicated when he discussed "the world within", what he called the "thing-in-itself."

The greatest tragedy of modern man is his loss of his sense of respect. He has no respect for anything. He has no respect for his gods, for his parents, or for his country. We have forgotten the meaning of our values. To know the meaning of beauty or truth we need to activate our moral and spiritual sensitivities. Unless we cultivate those sensitivities, we are incapable of knowing the significance of subtle experiences. In our effort to acquire, aggrandize and indulge, we have almost lost these sensitivities. We have lost the quality of life. We ought to recover that sensitivity – the ability to enjoy and be happy. Bhagat Singh, the Indian Freedom Fighter, walked to the gallows with a happy mind. Would you or I be able to do that? The intelligence to be happy and moral sensitivity are important ways of knowing higher truths.

There are thus many ways of knowing. We need to cultivate all those ways of knowing. The joy that we get out of an ethical and honest way of living is much more than the gratification we get from an immoral, unethical, aggrandizing and selfish life. But where do we find that kind of education?

Finally, we have spiritual knowledge. How do you know Spirit? How do you know God? Of course, for an accomplished person, when he opens his eyes and sees the sunrise, the birds flying, the lotus blooming, the moonlight, fireflies weaving golden designs in the darkness of the night, he can see the glory of God. For a Tagore that is enough. Unfortunately for you and me that is not enough. We have to sensitize ourselves. How can we do that and know God? Particularly if logic is not enough, sense perception is not enough, and mere feeling and morality are not enough.

Knowledge through Words: *Sabda Pramana* and *Sravana*

Sabda pramana, "the words of enlightened people," is a means to know God. Words give you knowledge. Words create great experiences for you. Suppose I call you a stupid person, what will be your reaction? The chemistry of your whole body will change. Your heart starts palpitating. Your blood pressure goes up. Just one word creates a world of difference for you!

Suppose you were looking for Mr. Vasudevan in the Central

Secretariat. You have never met him before. You search for him everywhere. Not knowing where he is, you ask a gentleman who happens to be rushing by. If that stranger says that he himself is Mr. Vasudevan, the person you are looking for, what would be your feeling? You will experience a great relief. A simple word has given you knowledge as well as experience. Similarly, if I say that you are a beautiful person – even if you think that you are not that beautiful – what will be your response? When you know that at least one person recognizes you as beautiful, it peps you up. Your life juices start flowing. You experience an inner energy. Your adrenaline starts rushing and you feel that you are on top of the world – that is, until you meet the next person who comments negatively about your appearance! Words create experiences.

It is not only sensate perception that can create experiences; it is not only ethical values that can create experiences; words, too, can create experiences. In fact, our mind is full of words. We know through words, through right understanding of words. Often we don't use *sabda* in the proper way. Presently we use *sabda* – words – to condemn, to criticize and to dispirit the other person. Similarly, the more we read the newspaper and watch television the more depressed we become. The vocabulary of the media is very depressing. What do you read in the newspaper these days? If it is not bad news, it is no news. We have become addicted to depressing and repetitive news – a very dangerous and pathological state of mind. We are not responsive to good words. We have either forgotten or never learned how to appreciate positive words.

The Scriptures say that words can be used effectively. Our mind is made up of words. Take away all the words from life. Where will we be? Can we think? Can we talk? All possibilities suddenly vanish! Words are very important. Words are the only way to transform your molecular structure and thought processes. There is no other way – your doctor cannot perform an operation to change your thought. He can only change physical processes. You may become mad, but you cannot become *God* by means of surgery.

How do we explore our full potential? How can we undergo subtle changes on different levels of our personality? If you go to a *guru*, the first thing he will tell you is to chant the *mantra*, *Shivoham*, or *Aum Nama Shivaya*. What does *Shivoham* mean? It means, "I am Shiva; I am infinite Consciousness; I am infinite Bliss." Instead of saying "I am a useless person. I am an unemployed person and nobody can improve me," say "*Shivoham*." Saying *Shivoham* is not brainwashing. When you say *Shivoham*, your mind can think of higher levels of your self and you will be able to realize your True nature. Shiva is the one who dances all the time. To be Shiva is to be always enthusiastic. Shiva is a person who has plenty of energy, who never tires. To be a Shiva is not to put a snake around your neck, nor to have matted hair. What is necessary is to experience the enthusiasm of Shiva. If you can spontaneously smile, then you can be called Shiva. By constantly chanting and remembering the mantra "*Shivoham*," you undergo a molecular change. Your whole energy starts organizing itself around this word. It is a programme that you can install in your system. When you install this programme your

system will organize accordingly. Words like *Shivoham*, *Aum Nama Shivaya*, *Aham Brahma Asmi* or *Tat Twam Asi* can create a profound non-invasive change in you, without creating any side effect. Generally, what do you do when your energy is low? You take a couple of drinks and feel on top of the world, but for how long? Maybe for a few minutes, for half an hour! Thereafter, you continue to be the same old fool you were before. Maybe worse! Earlier you at least had a healthy liver. After the drinks your liver becomes weak. Or you smoke to become energetic. Thereby, you only give trouble to yourself and others. You might gain two hours of excitement; thereafter you regress. Smoking and drinking are invasive methods of finding pleasures *and* incurring their debilitating side effects, whereas, chanting *Shivoham* is a non-invasive method to uplift your system. It ennobles life. Words are *that* powerful.

We are entering into a world where words will be used with great effect. There is no other instrument necessary for self-transformation. Mind cannot be changed with instruments. No surgeon can perform an operation on your mind, though he might say that the mind is nothing but brain chemistry. With the use of words, great changes can be made in the mind. Words are going to be the means of self-transformation and transformation of the world, because the "world is nothing but an arrangement of energy in the form of words" – *namarupatmakam idam jagat*. We are increasingly becoming aware of the power of *mantra*, the power of words, and how words change our reality. What are advertisements but words with powerful messages. We just *buy* words.

Rishis discovered the power of words long back. Realization is possible through the right understanding of words. We will be using words for positive changes in the coming century in a big way. Words are the only way to change your mind, the only way to change your thought processes, your molecular and cellular structure – the flow of neuropeptides.

Sravana is listening to the words of a *guru* and allowing the words to work their way into you. God is described as *Sabda Brahman* – to be realized through the right understanding of words. The *guru* will explain to you the meaning of words and sentences that expound the identity of God and Self. To know God, your true nature and full potential, deeply listen. *Sravana* is the means of knowing God. Different people might offer other methods. Some may say that by sitting under a tree you will realize God, but you will not. You will only get some crow's droppings on your head! A few might say that by putting your feet in lukewarm water, closing your eyes and lifting your hands you will realize God. At the most, what you can get is a sensation going through your spine. That sensation is not knowing God; it is only a lukewarm water – induced god! Once you remove your feet from the water, the god will be gone too! A seesaw god cannot be God, not the ultimate happiness that is God. Those kinds of experiences cannot take you either to your profound depths or the sublime heights. They cannot be sacred. They cannot unfold your full potential.

How do you know God? You have to sit at the feet of a *guru*, a great person – a person who has understood and who can use words effectively. His words are *pramana*, a means of knowledge.

The Ability to Listen

The problem of modern man is his inability to listen. Everybody wants to speak. Nobody wants to listen. We have lost the capacity to listen. Once we have lost the capacity to listen, what is the use of anyone speaking? You think that your family does not understand you, that your children do not understand you. But have you tried to understand anyone? Do you make an effort to understand anyone? You hear only your own words, your own mental chatter and lose the ability to understand and empathize. You do not learn. You live as a moron throughout your life. You ought to appreciate the value of listening and retrieve the ability to listen effectively.

I am reminded of a great Buddhist story: A student went to his *guru* to learn about God, happiness, to learn about his spiritual potential. The *guru* said first the student needed to learn to listen, so he sent the student to the forest. The student spent three years in the forest before returning to his *guru*. Then *guru* asked, "What did you hear in the forest?" The student replied, "I listened to the roar of the lions, the trumpeting of elephants, the rumble of the waterfalls, the landslides and thunder." The *guru* said, "But there is nothing special in hearing these! You can't avoid hearing the thunder! You have not listened carefully." And the student was sent back to forest and told to return after another five years. When he came back after five years his *guru* asked the same question, "What did you hear in the forest?" The student replied, "I heard the sweet music of the flower blossoming, the morning sun licking the dew from the grass, the wind playing through the bamboo forest and stars silently coming and taking their positions in the sky." The *guru* replied, "Now you are ready for learning – you will be able to listen to the soft whisper of the Spirit and the grandeur and glory of your own Self." The student had gained the sensitivity to listen.

Sravana is the ability to listen, not only to your teacher but also to the whole universe. Then you have the ability to remain sane in this crazy world. When you chant a *mantra*, when you listen to the words of the scripture – whether it is the *Bible*, the *Koran* or the *Bhagavad Gita* – your mind becomes quiet, because you are sensitive to words that have been formed in the seat of meditation, in revelation. When you listen and reflect upon those words, knowledge comes as a revelation. As it is said in the *Bible*, after Christ's baptism in the River Jordan, the sky split and the dove of peace descended and entered into His soul. Once you have that revelation, you yourself become a transformed person. Whatever you *speak* will be wisdom. Your *look* will have a healing power, and your *touch* will transform people. We need that ability to listen, to receive the revelation that is constantly happening, the revelation that made a simple shepherd boy, Kalidasa, into a great poet and scholar. Divine grace – the whisper of God – is the ultimate means of knowing.

Three

The Enlightened Person

STHITAPRAJNA

Cosmic religious feeling: the emotional state that one experiences when one recognizes the futility of human desires and the sublimity and marvellous order which reveals itself, both in nature and in the world of thought.

Albert Einstein

Understanding is a function of the dynamics of the knower, instruments of knowing and the object that impacts the subjective consciousness. These three components together create knowledge, experience, and worlds of realities – spiritual, mental, and physical. It is difficult, and often futile to pinpoint a ground reality, outer or inner, as unalterable truth. It is a flowing, wiggly swaying Truth, an open-ended participatory reality. God has many faces and enlightenment is multi-dimensional.

How do we understand what knowledge is, and how is knowledge conditioned by the means of knowing? How to distinguish between right and wrong knowledge (*prama* and *bhrama*), imaginary and real knowledge (*sankalpa* and *pramana/pratyaya*), non-knowledge and trans-knowledge (*ajnana* and *prajnana*)? We ought to know all these nuances in the cognitive process in order to make right choices regarding knowledge, means of knowledge, and our values and goals in life.

Experiential Knowledge

One of our fundamental desires is to expand the arena of our knowledge. Living means to expand knowledge. Nobody can be happy with ignorance, although sometimes we say, "Ignorance is bliss" – sometimes it is better *not* to know. Suppose you come to know what your good friend actually thinks of you; you may be in for a shock. Though we may think that ignorance is blissful, nobody feels comfortable with ignorance. We are born with ignorance. We are also born with the ability to know, but most of us do not use that ability fully and properly. For the total fulfillment of our personality, it is important that we apply many means of cognizing.

Not only do we want to know, we want to experience. Mere intellectual knowledge is not enough for us. Knowledge should change our worldview and lifestyle. It should give us a better and more wholesome way of experiencing life. Take, for example, the simple instance of a sunrise. Our ancients thought that the Sun rose in the east, travelled around the Earth and then dipped into the western horizon. But according to our present knowledge, it is not the Sun that travels around the Earth but the Earth that orbits around the Sun. While it revolves around the Sun, the Earth rotates on its own axis, creating for us the experience of day and night. It takes one year for the Earth to revolve around the Sun. With the change in our knowledge about this phenomenon, our perceptions about sunrise and seasons have also changed. Along with new perceptions, the manner in which we look at and experience the world also changes. The way we draw experience from our encounter depends upon our overall worldview.

Knowledge has to metamorphose into experience and ultimately give us the bliss of meditative Oneness. Knowledge that does not lead to inner joy is worthless. It is only organized ignorance. Hence the *Gita* says, "A knowledgeable person is a happy person." Knowledge and unhappiness cannot go together. This is the first teaching of Lord Krishna in the *Bhagavad Gita*. Wrong knowledge (*bhrama*) leads to discontent, and right knowledge (*prama*) blossoms into realization (*prajnana*).

In the second chapter of the *Gita*, the Lord says, "One who has awakened to the fullness of the Self is not tormented by grief." Knowledge is happiness. Unfortunately, in the modern world, the more we know the unhappier we become. The more we read newspapers and watch television the sadder we feel. As a result, sometimes we choose not to know, to be left alone – all by ourselves.

Such morbidity leads to pain, agony and grief. The Lord assures us in the *Bhagavad Gita*, "Enlightened people don't grieve" – *n'anusocanti panditah* (*Gita* II.11). Their self-awareness is free from ignorance, desire and conflict. Conflict is the cause of sorrow. Ignorance (*ajnana*) is dispelled by knowledge gained through the right means of knowing (*pramana*).

Holistic Perceptions

There are many ways of knowing. We use our sense organs. Using our sense organs we are able to distinguish between a wall and a door. Suppose you have no way of distinguishing a wall from a door and you try to walk through the wall. What happens? You end up with a bump on your forehead and may lose one or two teeth! Then you realize that you did not use your God-given faculty of sight. If somebody gives you a fruit, the first thing you do is to smell it. Does it smell good? You look at it, touch it, and if your sense organs say, "All right, it's edible," you eat it. You use your sense organs to negotiate your way through the labyrinth of physical life.

Not only do we use our sense organs, but we also use our rational faculty – a second way of knowing. Sense organs cannot give us the knowledge of subtle and temporal relationships. To ascertain the chain of causation, we have to use our logical and rational faculty. For example, the moment you see smoke, your reasoning powers infer that there is fire and you should take action to extinguish the fire. If smoke comes billowing from your house, although you have not seen the fire, you decide – rationally – to call the fire department.

We also have moral faculties – a third way of knowing. After all, what is morality? Morality is the ability to choose your responses keeping in mind the consequences of your actions, thoughts and intentions. Your choice of action is determined by the consequences that you want to generate. You exercise conscious control over innate impulses to channelize your energy towards fulfillment of worthy goals. Such control that you exercise is a moral act. For example, smoking a cigarette is pleasurable. At the same time you know that smoking causes unacceptable consequences. So you give up smoking as a moral discipline. If your neighbour is under hardship, you feel a momentary vicarious pleasure. But your moral sense also pricks you. You realize his present difficulties may visit *you* tomorrow, that all of us are invisibly connected! Taking secret pleasure in another's grief will invite the same upon your self, an unsavoury consequence. Therefore, you use your moral power to exercise restraint on harmful thoughts. Human beings are capable of developing and using their moral faculties provided they are educated in ethics. Education, in its fullest sense, means to bring out your moral and ethical faculties. It is another mode of learning and knowing.

The fourth way of knowing is through *sabda pramana* – learning from wise men, learning from scripture, using words as a means of knowing. A *mantra* – a verbal formula chanted for a particular effect – can purify, to a certain extent, our faculties of knowing. Whereas a *Mahavakya* – the great pronouncements of enlightened sages – faithfully listened to, deeply reflected and consistently meditated upon, leads to Self-knowledge and spiritual freedom.

Direct Revelation: *Anugraha*

The ultimate way of knowing is through *anugraha* – "grace" -- the factor of blessing, revelation, breakthroughs and intuition. Patanjali calls ultimate knowledge *rtambhara prajna* – "knowledge resonating with the rhythm and harmony of existence" (*Yoga Sutras* I:48). Grace comes as a "shower of blessings" – *dharma megha samadhi* – from the Lord, the Supreme *Guru* (*Yoga Sutras* IV:28). We all have had an occasional experience of grace in the darkest moments of our lives – a sudden flash lightning illumining the valley of life.

Informed use of these means of knowing – to understand the matter-mind-Spirit levels of our existence and organizing our interactive life accordingly – is the path to God. If we don't avail all these faculties, life remains incomplete, our experience of happiness shatters. Our faculties unused, disused and abused, we become sick – a result of not using our full potential of sensory, rational, moral, ethical and trans-sensory perceptions. Unfortunately, eating and sleeping are the minimum required for survival for seventy or eighty years before you exit, or are kicked out of, this world!

When you utilize all your faculties, all the doors of perception open and the walls isolating your individuality collapse. Knowledge and wisdom stream into you from all directions. In that state you can be called an *enlightened* person, a wise man – a *sthitaprajna*. Like opening the windows of your house – sunlight and fresh air rush in and you feel good. If you close all your doors and windows, the sunlight and breeze are shut out and you feel confined. You can't see the sky. Your life also becomes constricted and, as a result, you feel miserable. We need to open all the doors of perception so that we harvest the maximum from life and make life an experience of abundance – an orchestrated symphony, *nada Brahma*.

We all want to become whole and complete. For that, all doors of perception have to be kept open – not only the door of your sense organs, not only the door of your rational faculty, not only the door of your ethical and moral sensitivity, but also the door of your spiritual dimension. The whole of existence should openly communicate with you, and, for this, reflection on the scripture and meditation on the Self are mandatory.

You can open these doors in a multitude of ways: by daily practise of *pranayama*, by chanting a *mantra* or by an act of compassion. You can fast and change the avenues of your perception. You pick up an ant that has fallen into the water, and, disregarding its bite, put it safely on the ground. You feel so contented. Haven't you experienced it? Of course, there are people who let the ant die and feel a kind of mean pleasure. That is the lowest form of happiness. Even by planting and nourishing a tree you can open doors of perception. These ways of living can be easily be put into practise to give you a fresh view of life.

Eyes of Tradition

Gurus advocate a process of *sravana*, *manana* and *nididhyasana* – listening, reflecting and meditating on the Immutable Self as the path to Self-realization (*Brhadaranyaka Upanishad* IV.v.6). Vedanta suggests various steps to invoke higher faculties: *viveka* –

discrimination, *vairagya* – dispassion, and *abhyasa* – Self-abidance.

In the *Yoga Sutras*, Patanjali lists eight steps for *yogic* communion: *yama* and *niyama*, meaning ethical discipline and moral practices; *asana*, physical discipline; *pranayama*, physiological controls; *pratyahara*, detachment; *dharana*, concentration; *dhyana*, contemplation; and *samadhi*, immersion (*Yoga Sutras* II:29). Another sage, Narada, discusses *bhakti* (devotion) as a means to God-realization. He defines *bhakti* as *paramaprema* – meaning "supreme, unconditional love for the Lord" (*Narada Bhakti Sutra* I:2). The *Lord* can mean a chosen deity or a composite of all noble values – i.e., *satya*, *prema* and *dharma* – truthfulness, love and righteousness. When you develop a deep affinity for these values, your cognitive scope expands to encompass the whole of existence.

In Chapter 13 of the *Gita* twenty values are given beginning with *amanitvam* – egolessness, *adambhitvam* – non-pretentiousness, etc. (XIII:7–11). All these are disciplines for Self-transformation. Use them and improve the quality of your cognitive faculties. Discover your true Self and enrich your experience. Then you will know the boundless bliss that you have always been.

In the previous chapter, we discussed the myriad possibilities of fresh cognitions, new experiences and ways of enjoying life, not just in terms of comforts but by unfolding your potential and discovering who you are – your depths, your profundity, your grandeur and glory. These are possible provided you make some effort towards your goal. Initially, your *tamas* – dullness – has to be overcome. That is why the *guru* has to be with you, to bang on your head and twist your ear – awaken you from the deep slumber: *pramado vy mrytyu* – "heedlessness is death!"

Calamity, Opportunity and Human Destiny

Krishna admonished Arjuna, "Your confusion and lack of energy are due to your Self-ignorance!" Arjuna wanted to run away from the challenges of life. Who runs away from a challenge? One who doubts his capabilities and lacks energy! The same challenge that brings calamity to one person presents an opportunity for another. When you explore your full potential, the world becomes an interesting challenge, a field in which to express your infinitude and bliss. What would such a beatific life be like? How do you gain that freedom and flexibility? You are eager to find answers to these questions because such a state seems to be your ultimate destiny.

We all have our ideals. When we were teenagers, our ideal was the film star whom we imitated. As we grew up, politicians or musicians or painters were our ideals. As we mature our ideal becomes the *wise person*, someone the *Gita* calls a *sthitaprajna*. In the immemorial past, during our endless wandering life in the jungle, the fittest and the strongest survived. Now, in the modern information jungle, the wisest survive: "The wise shall inherit the earth; the wise shall live happily." Who is that wise person? Can you describe him? What is the ultimate end of humankind? To become wise or foolish? To become a Buddha or a bum? What is our destiny? At one time or another all of us confront thoughts about destiny.

Who am I? What is my destiny? What am I to become? As

human beings, where are we bound? These are very interesting questions. Of course, most of us say that, ultimately, we will wind up as nothing more than corpses. All the strong men, all the knowledgeable people, all the great warriors and conquerors – where have they ended up? In the burial ground or on the next pyre! Is that my destiny, too? These questions loom large in the mind.

According to the *Bhagavad Gita* the destiny of man is to become wise like a Buddha, compassionate like a Jesus Christ, and dynamic like Krishna. But some people don't agree with this proposition. They think that the destiny of man is to decompose like a vegetable – "I come from vegetable and return to vegetable!" A few others think that man is a product of God's workshop, and that God is experimenting with several designs. Some other group thinks that man is only a link in the chain of evolution and that *superman* is yet to evolve. Yet another hypothesis is that we will encounter extraterrestrial intelligence and a new species will arise out of that intercourse. Are we just one link in the evolutionary chain that nature will later discard in preference to something greater? Maybe if we tamper with our genetic sequence a new monstrous trait or gene could come about by accident or mutation! There is so much to imagine and fear about human destiny!

An Ideal Person: The *Sthitaprajna*

In the battlefield of Kurukshetra, Arjuna asked Lord Krishna to describe the ideal person, a profile of a *sthitaprajna*. He wanted to know: "Does such a person have any relevance to my destiny? If so, how can I, like him, maximize my self? How can I actualize the highest ideal of creation? How can I become an accomplished, complete person? Give me a thumbnail picture of the ideal person so that I can meditate on that image. If I am deficient in some values, I will cultivate those values. If I have to chant a *mantra* one million times a year, I will do that also. My purpose in life is to become a *sthitaprajna*!" These dreams and questions circulate in our mind, consciously or unconsciously, as we speculate answers.

The word *sthitaprajna* itself is very meaningful: *sthita* means "steady," *prajna* means "knowledge." A *sthitaprajna* is one who has gained "steady knowledge" – Self-knowledge. He is neither distracted nor disturbed. His wisdom is steady, stable. Another word used for *sthitaprajna* is *samadhistha* – one who is rooted in *samadhi*, centred in the Self. *Samadhi* is a state of being. So how do you describe a person who is in *samadhi*, whose knowledge is steady, whose wisdom is abiding? Arjuna's question to Krishna was,

> *Sthita-prajnasya ka bhasa samadhi-sthasya, Kesava*
> *sthita-dhih kim prabhaseta kim asita vrajeta kim?*

"How will a wise man speak? How will he sit? How will he walk? How does he move about in this world? How do you recognize a man of wisdom?" (*Gita* II:54).

The popular notion is that an enlightened person lives lost in a higher world, beyond the reach of ordinary mortals. He refrains from speaking, always absorbed in meditation seated cross-legged in *padmasan*. And, our fear is, "What if I have arthritis? I won't be able to sit continuously in *padmasan* and enjoy *sthitaprajnatvam*!" It seems to be an impossible ideal for a man in the world. Arjuna was a man of action, a *ksatriya* or warrior. He had never in his life learned to sit in *padmasan*, and, suddenly, if he were to be asked to sit cross-legged, and so become a *sthitaprajna*, it might not have been possible. Is this state of *samadhi* contingent upon the way you sit? Is it contingent upon the way you walk? Arjuna desperately wanted a description of a *sthitaprajna*, this ideal person's daily life, his capacities and limitations, his behavioural and response patterns. In short, snapshots of the wise man in flesh and blood, engaged in his daily chores.

I have heard people bragging, "O, my *Guruji* is a *sthitaprajna*. He can speak many languages, even Chinese and Japanese. He simply chooses not to speak those languages!" In other words, all his knowledge remains unmanifest! Arjuna wasn't seeking such vague answers. His questions were pragmatic. He wanted to know how a *sthitaprajna* responded in actual situations: "How does he conduct himself? How does he organize his behavior?" Arjuna did not want any false claims about *sthitaprajna*. Anyone can make claims! "I am always in *samadhi*." "I am *Brahman* and see everyone as my Self!" But what happens when his claim is challenged? Suppose somebody calls him a donkey. How will he respond? Will he kick him with his hind legs and prove that he is a donkey? It is of paramount importance how you respond! Don't make any claims. Your claims of your steadiness are proven by the way you respond, by the way you talk, by the way you sleep, eat and relate with others.

Arjuna was a practical phenomenologist. He wanted to know *how* he should respond and *how* he could bring out his full potential, *how* he could bring out the ideal person from within. In the *Bhagavad Gita*, Krishna says that the greatest quality of an enlightened person is that he does not grieve under any circumstance. An enlightened person, a wise person, a *sthitaprajna* "does not grieve" – *n'anusocanti panditah* (II:11). He does not worry over anything.

Grief and worry are very debilitating emotions that make us helpless. When we grieve we are unable to respond adequately to situations, to fully engage ourselves in activity. Freedom from worry is the hallmark of an enlightened person.

Descriptions of the Ideal Person

Various words are used in the *Bhagavad Gita* to describe an ideal person. *Sthitaprajna* is one word. *Yogi* is another word. *Bhakta* is yet another word. The *sthitaprajna*, *yogi* or *bhakta* have unique qualities in common, which make them ideal. Who is a *bhakta*, a devotee? He is "a person who does not hate anybody and who loves the whole world" – *Advesta sarva bhutanam maitrah karuna eva ca* (XII:13). You cannot be a *bhakta* if you say that you are in love with Lord Krishna but hate your neighbour, Krishnaswami!

Bhakti means loving the entire creation, giving and receiving love. When you give and don't *receive*, your giving is out of arrogance. In such cases, the ego of the giver cripples the self-esteem of the receiver. Therefore, allow the receiver the opportunity to give something in return. What is necessary is give *and* take. Those who give love receive love. Love fosters mutuality. Some people only give and make the receiver feel wretched. Some people only take and, of course, make the giver feel empty. Through the process of give and take we create a flow of energy, synergy and affluence in our interaction. This is the meaning of love. To be a *bhakta* or a *yogi* is not easy. At the same time, we can say being a *bhakta* is *either* difficult *or* easy depending upon how you view it! In the *Gita*, Chapter 14, Krishna uses the word *gunatita* for *sthitaprajna* – "One who has gone beyond the play of *gunas*, who does not react to guna-influenced modifications of mind." The *gunatita* enjoys the freedom to play with the three modes of psychic energy. So, let me remind you, all these words point to the same idea – whether you use the word *yogi*, *sannyasi*, *sthitaprajna*, *samadhistha* or *gunatita*.

Yoga and Desirelessness

"A *yogi* is one who works without expectation" – *Anasritah karma-phalam karyam karma karoti yah / sa samnyasi ca yogi ca na niragnir na c'akriyah* (VI.1). "The *yogi* works as a happy person and not *for* happiness." Most of us work for happiness and still we don't attain happiness. If you work happily then you are a *sannyasi* or a *yogi*.

Where is the seat of desire? The seat of desire is your own heart. When you are able to go beyond desire, when you are able to renounce desire, then, through the purity of heart you become Self-realized. Krishna says,

> *Prajahati yada kaman sarvan, Partha, mano-gatan*
> *atmany evatmana tustah sthita-prajnas tado'cyate*

"A wise man renounces desire, he finds his repose in the Self" (II.55). It is difficult to accept the above proposition that one can be totally free from desire. You may say, "If that is the case, I'm the last person to go for wisdom," because renouncing desire is impractical. In fact, can we totally renounce desire? We must at least have the desire to get out of bed in the morning or to leave a hall at the end of a lecture! If we renounce such desires, we will all be stuck in bed or glued to a chair! Desire is the engine of all action. We are immobile without desire. We know that if we don't act, we will not grow. So, what does *renouncing desire* mean? Does it mean suppressing desire? Suppression of desire may be possible, but is it desirable? We can *pretend* that we have no desires. When asked whether you would like a cup of coffee you can pretend and say "No," whereas you really wish to have one. If you suppress your desire, you become a hypocrite. You may look like a holy man, but inwardly you are hollow.

Then what does renouncing desire mean? Is it a state of absolute desirelessness? Is it repressing desire and creating a vast basement of discontent and stinking reactions in the mind? Can anybody renounce the desire to *grow*, the desire to *act*, and the desire to *serve*? In fact, we grow by pursuing desires. If we have no desire, we don't grow. So then, what else could we mean by the renunciation of desire?

Two Kinds of Desire

The misunderstanding of the word *renunciation* is the root cause of misinterpretation of our tradition, degradation of our religion, and intellectual ambivalence towards spiritual disciplines. The two kinds of desires are: 1) the desire to have – to procure things which we don't have (*yoga*), and preserve things which we already have (*kshema*); and, 2) the desire to be one's Self, to be unconditionally happy. This second desire presents a contradiction, for how can I desire to be myself? Desire is an outward projection of your energy. The object of desire is always *other* than you. You can desire an object that exists only as *other* than yourself. Is it not true? Will you desire a head over your shoulders? You don't desire a head on your shoulders because one is already there! You desire whatever you *don't* have, that which is *other* than yourself.

Desire is always an outward movement. There must be an object for you to desire. The object could be a person, a place, a situation, a word, a look, a touch – anything. Sometimes you desire a touch. Sometimes you desire a glance. Sometimes you desire a nice word. If nobody speaks a kind word to you then you are disappointed. Whatever may be the object of your desire, it is always desire for an external object, for something from a source outside yourself. Is it not? Once you desire an object, the next problem is that you want to possess it. Suppose you go to a bookstore and see a recently published book that you want to buy. But since you have no money you leave without making the purchase. The book keeps coming to mind, until finally, one day, you make a special trip to purchase the book that lingered so long in your mind.

Desire derives from a sense of incompleteness. For example,

you attend a marriage party, and you are served free food including free ice cream! Since your friend is paying for it and you don't have to spend your hard-earned money, you eat till you are stuffed to the gills. Your desire for food is well satisfied. Your only desire now is altruistic – to serve those who have not eaten and enjoy seeing them all eating! An incomplete person is a victim of desire, and a complete person is a master of desire. Completeness is not opposed to desire. On the contrary, a complete person integrates desire as a means of self-expression.

I am reminded of another story: A couple went to a marriage party and others noticed the husband frequently visiting the ice-cream counter. His wife was annoyed by her husband's behaviour and asked him, "Aren't you ashamed of taking so many servings of ice cream? Others are talking about you!" Her husband replied, "Don't worry, dear. Whenever the waiter asked me who the ice cream was for, I just told them it was for you!" Not only was that man feeling incomplete but he was projecting his sense of incompleteness upon another.

Re-possessing Completeness

Desires, which make you run towards objects, are born of a sense of incompleteness. Like having a stone in your shoe, you are uncomfortable, unable to *live* with a sense of incompleteness. We think we will feel complete either after obtaining an object that we like or getting rid of an object that we dislike. But what does experience teach us? Do we feel a sense of wholeness after possessing or dispossessing objects? No, we have other desires – all due to our feelings of incompleteness, our Self-ignorance. Like a train carrying cargo, we keep on adding more and more to our stock of possessions and then have to drag the whole load. That is why sometimes people have heart attacks – they carry the heavy load on and on.

Though desire is always for an object, we don't actually desire the object *per se*, because, later we dislike the very same object. We dislike the place that we once loved. We detest the ideology to which we once subscribed. Two lovers, who write letters in blood, later draw each other's blood! Why? Because energies change, interests change, ideologies change. We get bored and need a change. The object we desired initially has lost its charm, and other desires take its place. We don't desire a particular object for its own sake. Actually, we seek something other than what objects can give. The object is only a form, a shadow of the *Real*. We are looking for something enduring, beyond the object. Can you identify what that is?

The rishis discovered what we seek. *We seek Happiness*. By procuring objects of desire, indulging in the object, we are really seeking union with the Self – which is Happiness. When we are complete all by ourselves, we are happy. We experience no further desire. Have you ever noticed that possession of an object of your desire brings a temporary freedom from desire and a momentary sense of completeness or satisfaction? What we actually seek is a *permanent* freedom from desire – a desireless state of Self-abidance. When we are free from desire there is no extroverted movement, the mind doesn't project (*sankalpa*). Like a child, tired of his toys, turns to his mother and collapses in her loving arms, we centre in the lap of Happiness.

What you seek – beyond objects and persons and situations and ideologies – is a desireless state, an inner fullness and Self-abidance. This state of inner joy is impossible for an extroverted person to attain. Pleasure leads to pain. Therefore, Krishna says, an intelligent person understands this and tries to discover happiness *within*.

The Nature of Happiness

Happiness is neither in the object, nor in thought, nor in ideology, nor in Heaven, nor in pleasure of any sort. Happiness is your *svarupa*, your innate *nature*. When you know this, you will decide to be happy *with*, *without*, or *in spite* of everything. You just *decide* to be happy right here, right now! Earlier, you chose to be unhappy – due to your notion that happiness depended upon extraneous factors. When you know that your true nature is happiness you become wise and, for the first time, realize that no one or no situation can *make* you either happy or unhappy. You sit down, relax, close your eyes, watch your thoughts and go beyond in an experience of inner joy. Unless you are happy *by* yourself, in yourself, *as* yourself, there is no hope of attaining enduring Happiness.

Once you are wise – realize inner joy – you joyously relate with everyone. Thereafter, relationships undergo a qualitative change. You can even relate with a criminal, because not even a criminal can manipulate you. When you are unhappy, people can manipulate you – for example, you will do anything for someone who says, "You're a wonderful person!" But if you are a self-rooted person, no one can manipulate you with sugarcoated words! If you are content nobody can worm his way into your heart and disturb your life.

In the *Gita*, Krishna asks us to renounce our desire for happiness. When we renounce our desire for happiness, we announce that our *nature* is happiness. These are two sides of the same coin. When we announce that we are happy, happiness is there to bless us. As you think, so you are! You realize that you are not useless, only *used less* – that your vast potential is waiting to be tapped!

Happiness is instantaneous and experienced in the present. Otherwise, *when* will we be happy? A person thinks, "When I complete my studies I'll be happy." But even after he finishes his studies he continues to be unhappy. Then he contemplates, "Well, I was wrong, but now my job will make me happy!" Is he happy after getting a job? No, because he has been sent to a remote village where he has to take bath in the open. Then he thinks, "Marriage will bring me happiness!" Does marriage make anyone happy? Do we have the self-worth necessary for a successful marital relationship?

An incomplete person is always insecure. He becomes possessive. How can anyone be happy in a possessive relationship? When his marriage falters, he looks forward to being happy after his children were born, because then, at least, he hears his children's sweet prattling. Are you happy after children were born? No, because you seldom get any sleep with their constant crying. Then we think, "When the children grow up and get a job and start earning, they'll make me happy." And until they grow up, you sweat and toil for them. As they become teenagers, all your problems become intensified because of their bad habits – they go out in the middle of the night and if you ask them where, they say, "It's none of your business." After they return, if you ask them, "Why you are so late?" they reply, "Stop interfering!" Then you postpone being happy until after your children get married. After their marriage you end up babysitting your grandchildren! After long years of marriage, when your children and grandchildren have grown up and are living elsewhere, a stony silence looms between you and your partner. You just look at each other's vacant gaze – with nothing to say or to fight about. You postponed your happiness all these years. When *are* you going to be happy? Decide right now that you *are* a happy person. Relate happily *with* others and not for happiness.

Happiness and Intelligence

Acceptance of these facts is the first condition of intelligence. Don't look to others for your happiness. This is the first expression of intelligence, the realization, "I don't have to depend upon anybody to be happy; happiness is my nature." It takes supreme intelligence – an intelligence far beyond even Einstein's – to understand that you can be happy *by* yourself.

That is why Krishna says, "He is a wise man who can be spontaneously happy." Once true happiness is attained, desire disintegrates. A person who has eaten to his fullest has no desire for more food. Krishna says, *Atmany evatmana tustah*. "One who is happy by himself, in himself, remains happy under all conditions" (II:55). A wise man is happy within himself – why is it so? It is because of the clarity of his thought! Intelligence is an ability to perceive things as they are. It is an ability to do things with minimum effort. An intelligent person is naturally and effortlessly happy.

Effortlessness is the defining quality of intelligence. An unintelligent person makes all kinds of effort, but without any result. He burns the midnight oil, but when the exam results come, he's way below the mark. Another person may have only read his text once, but with great concentration, and he scores 95 percent! In one glance an intelligent person understands and solves the problem, effortlessly. An intelligent person is always relaxed. An unintelligent person is always tense – he has no time for anyone or anything. Whereas, an intelligent person finds time for everything.

Intelligence and Steady Wisdom

Intelligence means a relaxed existence, a relaxed way of being and doing. You need not *have* or *do* anything to be a happy person. When you are happy and intelligent, the whole of nature works for you, offering her bounties at your feet. To whom does the bank advance loans? Not to a beggar! But if you have security, if you have some property, then the banker is ready to advance a sizeable loan. When you are happy, everyone dances around you. If you are unhappy, everyone shuns you. Isn't that your experience?

The *Bhagavad Gita* teaches abiding wisdom. Wisdom is not accumulated information but rather instantaneous Self-realization.

What is the nature of that steady knowledge, that wisdom? It is doubt-free abiding knowledge that one's nature is happiness. *Anandoham*. No experience, outer or inner, can disturb that knowledge. You may be poor or rich; you may be knowledgeable or ignorant; you may be powerful or powerless; the crux of the matter is your rootedness in the Self. Always hold on to the knowledge, "I am happy." Then nothing matters – neither your surroundings, nor your possessions or your relations – none of these add to, or subtract from, your happiness.

Even if the situation is hostile, your happiness remains undisturbed. The *Gita* says,

> *Duhkhesu anudvigna-manah sukhesu vigata-sprhah*
> *vita-raga-bhayakrodhah sthita-dhir munir ucyate*

"Neither tormented by grief nor longing for pleasure, they live free from lust, fear and anger, established in the Self!" (II:56). *Duhkha* means "an unpleasant environment." People may praise or criticize, but praise does not increase your happiness nor does criticism decrease your happiness. You no longer either crave or recoil from situations. All situations are right for you. Preferences you may have, but extreme likes and dislikes are shed. Nothing influences the quantum, or the quality, or experience of your happiness.

Detachment and Steady Wisdom

The wise person is free from the debilitating emotion of *raga*, that is, "clinging attachment." There are people who cling since they are *so* lonely and *so* depressed, *so* unhappy and *so* low in self-esteem! They look for someone onto whom they can cling. Be compassionate towards such people! Don't we ourselves cling to our children, not allowing them to go anywhere? In our clinging we stunt their growth. Why is it so? Are we such insecure people? We are strangulating rather than loving them. How do we rid ourselves of this kind of insecurity and lack of trust in ourselves and in others? How do we acquire the freedom to allow another's space and identity?

Where there is attachment there is fear. Fear makes us ignore our principles and tell lies, lose our self-discipline and betray our standards. All your fears, bad dreams and omens appear when there is attachment. Whenever there is anger understand that it is due to unfulfilled desires. An Enlightened person is one who is naturally happy, free from attachment, free from fear and anger.

These are the three debilitating forces – attachment, fear and anger – working in our psyche disallowing the expression of our *true* nature – *Satchidananda*, Infinite Bliss. Overcome these three negative forces to have a natural self-expression of happiness in all relationships.

Centredness

Krishna leaves aside the metaphysical aspects of "steady wisdom," offering instead a pragmatic, behavioural description of a wise person. A *sthitaprajna* is one who is comfortable with himself. Once you are comfortable with yourself, you become eternally playful and transcend your limitations. You easily come to terms with your relationships, your physicality, your thoughts and your unconscious. You effortlessly manage your *karmic* load. If you are a happy person, anything can be managed effectively. If you are an unhappy person, you become a victim of the immediate situation and its long-term consequences! If you don't know how to ride the bicycle that was gifted to you, the bicycle is a burden. Attached to the wonderful gift, you can't give it up and yet you don't know how to ride it, so it sits under the staircase! Such a dilemma can only be a sure source of pain. If you know how to ride, when you receive the bike, you thank your benefactor profusely!

Krishna says that all instrumentalities – the body-mind complex that you have fashioned over a long evolutionary period – become *either* a burden *or* an opportunity. Provided we have the rootedness, we will be able to use these instruments, just as with a lever and foothold to stand one can lift the entire weight of the world.

One who has no centre is called an "eccentric," meaning "off – centre," "imbalanced." According to modern psychologists, all of us have neuroses. The psychologist himself is a neurotic! Hence, there is no objective standard for mental health in the first place! Once you find your own centre, you will be a balanced person. How do you know that you are centred? Suppose that your job requires you to leave your native land and go to the United States of America. In America you might be staying in five-star hotels with all possible comforts, but still you anxiously look forward to returning home. Home is your centre – where you abide peacefully. Ultimately when you reach home, you give a sigh of relief, "Now I'm home!"

whether you live in a palace or a hut. Similarly, we have to come back to our real home – the Self. Hurry Home! *Hari OM*!

It is this sense of comfort, relaxation and security that we want. Due to his rootedness in the Self, a *wise man* has all this and more. So, find your rootedness. A person who is centred is also wise – the paragon of happiness, the standard of life and health. For the modern "schizophrenic" individual, this discovery is of paramount importance in order to regain wholeness and indivisible individuality. We begin our *true* life thereafter. Until that discovery, life is only a mad running around. There is no centre at all. After reaching your centre you can love the world and lead a productive life.

Only a happy person, who loves the world, has the intelligence to know that if he hurts somebody the hurt will boomerang. If I insinuate something negative about another person, it comes back to me. Other people mirror our faces. The *other* is like a wall against which things echo and rebound. A wise person is supremely intelligent, happy by himself, lives in loving relationship with the world. He also is a productive person. After all what is productivity? It is something new and unique that you contribute. Only when we are happy can we become creative and productive.

When you gain these levels of intelligence, then your faculties unfold and you become a unique person. You do not imitate. Your contribution is immediate and original. You are the final flowering of existence. You are in partnership with God.

Four

Non-Reaction to the Fruits of Work

KARMA YOGA

Reconcile with God in faith;
Reconcile with fellow human beings in love.

St. Paul

We have been exploring the unique and wholesome characteristics of the enlightened person – the highest ideal that inspires humankind. By meditating on such a person we grow and reach our spiritual heights.

Revisiting the *Sthitaprajna*

The *sthitaprajna* consistently pursues excellence in his chosen field of activity. He is able to establish a loving relationship with his environment – a synergizing, sharing, caring fellowship with others. He also has this additional advantage of living in touch with the Spirit – the source of infinite energy.

There are people who are creative working alone but in company with others, working as a team, they become destructive. Indians are especially poor team players. The saying is "one Indian is equivalent to ten Japanese; but ten Indians make only one Japanese." In this turbulent society putting the ideal of *sthitaprajna* in practise can make top class political and business managers.

The *sthitaprajna* enjoys three levels of intelligence in his awareness: He is individually productive, integrates his individuality into the collectivity and, taps into Cosmic Intelligence. He is a fully developed human being. This is what we see in the character of Lord Krishna. He enjoyed debating Pandavas' war strategies as well as driving Arjuna's chariot. Are we capable of such fluidity? Our thoughts are, "How dare you ask me to drive your car! Who do you think I am?" We identify closely with our work, and, as a result, work and its outcome defines our attitude about ourselves, rather than our self-perception defining our attitude toward work and its outcome. Krishna did not feel defined by his work because he knew himself to be Infinite. He drove a chariot, tended the horses, and comforted the wounded and demoralized. In those days, the conduct of war was governed by rules of *dharma*. War ceased after sunset and warriors disengaged from battle. Krishna would then care for the horses and feed them, just as any other charioteer. From Krishna's example we understand that wise men enjoy varieties of work. No task is below their dignity.

Effortless Happiness

A *sthitaprajna* does not desire or work for happiness. Why doesn't he? Because he is already a happy person. When you exist as a happy person, then there is no need to desire happiness. The fish cannot die of thirst. Can you imagine a fish in the ocean thirsting for water? Impossible, because the fish is born and lives in water. Similarly, a wise person breathes and lives in the "ocean of happiness" – *Satchidananda sagara*.

When you have no desire for happiness, you are desireless happiness. In that state all your material desires will be naturally fulfilled. Then live beyond time and don't feel the pressure of work. Your mind is at rest. When you relax, things come to you on their own accord. When you seek a thing it runs away from you. You must have experienced this phenomenon. You wait for a particular bus, and that bus alone fails to turn up. All other buses come. So, the following day, you wait for some other bus and that bus alone does not come. All other buses drive up and stop, including the bus you waited for on the previous day. Because when you wait for the bus, it never arrives. When you desire something, it eludes you. When you give up your desire, the object appears before you. Desire is the cause of denial.

A wise person is free from desire in two ways. First, he does not desire happiness, because he has discovered himself to be the source of happiness. Second, since he is free from the desire for happiness, all his *other* desires get effortlessly fulfilled. Nature rolls at his feet with her bounties.

This is the ideal of a *sthitaprajna*, realization of which is possible for all of us. In the process of realizing this ideal, you face the struggles imposed by the limitations of material life – like fixing breakfast in the morning, washing your clothes, etc. How do you live through these daily struggles without forgetting your true nature? Living in this world as a happy person is the greatest challenge we humans face.

Analyzing "I"

When you say 'I,' the word refers to *you*, the subject. We use the word 'I' frequently. The subjective 'I,' the experiencer, is the centrepiece of all objective experience. The word 'I' is used to indicate several aspects of the personality.

According to *Upanishads*, the real meaning of the word 'I' is *Satchidananda*, the Infinite Spirit. A *guru* gives you *mantra upadesa*. *Mantra* is a formula of words to reach your own deep awareness, God. *Upadesa* is an advice upon which you have to reflect and meditate. The *upadesa* is encapsulated in the great *Mahavakya*: *Tat Tvam Asi* – "You Are That." We need to reflect upon this *Mahavakya* because it suggests an idea that is contrary to our daily experience. Instead of feeling, "I am an Ocean of Bliss," we often feel that we are a cesspool of pain and sorrow.

Although we use the word 'I' all the time, we don't understand the significance of the word. We don't have the real experience of 'I'. Our [illegible] lost somewhere amidst our experiences. When you say, "I am sitting on a chair," what is meant? Have you ever bothered to ask just *who* is that 'I' sitting on the chair? Through analysis you discover that your body is that which you are referring to as sitting on the chair, and that the chair is related only to the body. The chair is the *substratum* and the body is *substrated* upon the chair. Both the chair and your body are objects of awareness. They exist as thought modifications in the mind. Mind exists in Awareness.

What You Have, You Cannot Be

When you are in deep sleep, the mind is quiet and without thought. Then you are unaware of both your body and your environment. When thoughts arise, both body and objects come back into your awareness. When thought is absent, as when you are in deep sleep, there is no body and there are no objects. What do we understand from such an experience? Your body is a thought in your mind. People think unreflectively, "I am the body." But upon deeper enquiry we understand, "I am *not* the body; I *have* a body." There is a lot of difference between these two modes of understanding. Whatever you have or possess, *that* you are not. The real nature of the possessor transcends both the possessor as well as his possessions.

Our enquiry ought to be a reflection on the true meaning of 'I.' In fact, any religion's most profound purpose must be an enquiry into the meaning of this word – 'I.' This 'I' is the locus of all problems. And this same 'I' is the key to the solution of your problems. "*What* is your problem?" The feeling that "I am unhappy" is our main problem. If that problem is solved, then all the other problems will be solved. What do you seek ultimately? Happiness!

It is the ignorant 'I' that creates the thoughts: "I am inadequate;" "I am lonely;" "I am sad." These thoughts are like rocks tied to your ankle by a chain. You may initially walk a little ways, dragging the rocks along, but you can't walk properly and you become fatigued. And if you leap into that thought, it is like taking a leap into the turbulent river – the rocks will pull you down and down, and finally you will drown. If you loosen the chain and remove the rocks, you float to the top and swim safely ashore.

The thought, "I am unhappy" constantly bothers you. If you deeply enquire into such thoughts when they arise, you will understand that *you* are not really unhappy. On the contrary, you understand yourself to be an Ocean of Bliss.

Ordinarily, when we say 'I' we mean only the body-mind complex – our thoughts, our ambitions, our frustrations, our memories and our body identity. Everyone perceives his 'I' as a separated entity different from everything else. Our 'I,' like a flooded stream, overflows with thoughts, desires, impulses, fears, anxieties and hopes. We are only conscious of the 'I' with a physical structure – the historical 'I.' This body-oriented notion of our Self is called ignorance or impurity, which is the cause of desire-prompted work and work-related reactions.

That 'I' which serves as our frame of reference in the state of ignorance is the *conscious* subject. When someone speaks and you listen, you are *conscious* of the process. You are also a subject in contradistinction to the object. The table is an object, but you are a subject. In addition, those objects cannot objectify you. You are conscious of objects that are presented to your awareness. Therefore, you can say with assurance, "I touch," "I hear," "I think," etc. Even thought is an object presented to your consciousness.

Needs, Desires and Laws

All your needs were taken care of when you were in your mother's womb. You led a very protected life. As a baby you had natural, uncultivated needs, which your parents satisfied. By the age of twelve or thirteen you became self-conscious. Prior to that age you were *only* conscious and *not* self-conscious. When you became self-conscious, you started objectifying the world, seeing the world other than yourself. Then you became conscious of your thoughts, which enabled you to extrapolate thoughts and create a psychological world.

The psychological world is personal and private, whereas the objective world is interpersonal and public, a shared experience. For example, when two people look at a table both of them experience the same table. Our recognition corresponds to the table outside which conforms to the other person's perception of the table. However, from individual to individual, personal thoughts about the table vary.

By the age of twelve or thirteen, we develop our own psychological needs apart from our biological needs. When you have psychological needs, you dream, but you cannot live in dreams all the time. The main question is, how do you fulfill your psychological needs: your desire for success, your desire for recognition, and your desire for respect? A child has no desire for respect. Even if you call the child "silly," the child is happy, because, he or she does not know the meaning of that word. He will go around telling everyone that his mother called him "silly." A child is innocent.

First-level needs are biological needs and they are fulfilled naturally. Psychological needs are called "second-level needs." These second-level needs – the need for love, for attention, for respect, for identity, for being part of a larger organization or a larger structure, for power and control – are all *ego* needs. These are your own creation, your own imagination. That is why teenagers become demanding and rebellious. They have their own plans and don't brook any interference.

Earlier, as a baby, you were part of a whole. Now, with ego needs, you become a distinct person. Psychological needs make us real individuals, separate entities. Western culture promotes individual identity. Eastern culture tries to suppress this separate identity for the sake of the family or group identity. Each cultural emphasis has its own advantages and disadvantages. The promotion of individualism disrupts family life, causes antisocial behavior, violence and selfishness. The suppression of individual identity makes people sheepish, suicidal and manipulative, limits our personal options and stunts creativity and individual aspiration.

You can fulfill your psychological needs in a dream world, but fulfilling your dreams in the actual world requires conformity with certain laws. When you meet with obstacles, you see these laws in operation – physical and ethical laws. For example, as a child you didn't listen at first when your mother asked you not to put your hand into fire. But once you reach out and burn your fingertips, experience fire, you yourself will avoid the fire. You might even warn your mother, "Mom, don't put your finger in the fire!" Fire burns; it is a scientific law. At the same time, fire can be used for various beneficial purposes – to cook a meal, or to fire pottery, or bake bread, or to keep warm.

Emotional Intelligence

We know that physical events occur according to the laws of physics. Hence, we have to modify our desire-projects to suit these laws. You are constrained to apply certain restraints in the fulfillment of your desires. The restraints we apply upon our desires require emotional intelligence. They are also called value-application. Desires become value -added pursuits, which in today's language is called EQ or emotional intelligence. It is not that we give up all our desires – for food, water, etc. – but we apply values to prioritize our desires. We have to accept that all our desires cannot be fulfilled. For example, you may want to become the Prime Minister of your country, but how many people can become the Prime Minister – even in India where the Prime Minister changes every two months? As an intelligent person you have to give up some desires and entertain those that have the possibility of being fulfilled.

Realistic Goal-Setting

In your desire-fulfilling enterprises, the first law that you apply is based upon the knowledge that all your desires cannot be fulfilled.

This is the beginning of wisdom. It is very difficult to accept that all your desires cannot be fulfilled. Desires are limitless and the means of fulfilling them are limited. It is a simple economic problem: too many people with too many desires, chasing too few goods. In India we are trying to create the same standard of life that America enjoys. Imagine a US standard of living for all the six billion people of this world! America is only three percent of the world population, but to sustain its standard of living, it utilizes 25 percent of the world's resources and contributes 23 percent of the world's pollution. We may appreciate or deprecate the American lifestyle, but if we think that all the people of the world must have the same standard of living as Americans, we would bleed the world to death. The world would become a vast desert. In the *Gita* it is said, *Yajna – dana – tapah – karma na tyajyam iti c'apare* – "Use the meagre resources of the earth prudently" (XVIII:3). By the age of twenty or twenty-two we realize that all our desires cannot be fulfilled; therefore, as the saying goes, cut your suit according to the cloth.

The second law is that even if we fulfill a desire we may not be happy. The fulfillment of desire – success – is not a guarantee for happiness. In fact, some of the most successful people in the world are the most unhappy. Their agony, amidst success, is all the more poignant.

We all come to understand this law by the age of thirty or thirty-five. Everything is there: bank balance, children, wife, servants, car, etc. Then why are you unhappy? You might say, "*Guruji*, that is what I want to ask you!" You want an explanation for your unhappiness. It is the simple law. Hasn't anyone told you? Desire fulfillment is no guarantee for happiness.

The first law is that all our desires cannot be fulfilled. The second law is that fulfillment of desire is no guarantee for happiness. The third law is that even if you gain happiness from fulfilling a desire, that happiness will not be lasting.

Limitation and Choice

Our body is limited. Our powers are limited. Our knowledge is limited. Our abilities are limited. Being a limited being we are unable to execute our plans perfectly. Krishna says, *Sarv'arambha hi dosena dhumen'agnir iv'avrtah* – "There is no work which is totally defect-free" (XVIII:48). We can only optimize our efforts. We can do our work more or less successfully. But perfection is not possible in any enterprise. This situation is anxiety producing. We are anxious because of the uncertainty involved in work and the consequences of our efforts. As a limited conscious subject, our life's course is uncertain. We live in a world that is governed by objective laws. These can be physical laws, social laws and moral laws. Once that realization dawns, you become mature in your approach to life. Your realization may be something like: "I am not an all-powerful entity; I live in a particular environment; my environment operates according to physical laws; I have to understand those laws and submit to them; I have to harmonize my desires with my environment." A child is ignorant of such laws, but as he grows to maturity, he learns to organize his actions according to the laws or else suffer the consequences.

And, hence Krishna says in the *Gita*, *Karmany ev'adhikaras te ma phalesu* – "You have a right to choose your actions but not the result thereof" (II:47). You can choose a particular programme of action. You can decide to come to a *Gita* discourse, and stay there till the lecture is over. That choice is within your ability. You take a car or ride a bus (the means) to reach there. Whether you reach there or not is not within your control. On the way, for example, you meet a friend who asks you, "Where are you going?" Since you want to avoid telling him that you are going to listen to a *Gita* discourse, you evade an answer. Finally, you end up taking him home and never make it to the discourse you intended to hear! There are always unexpected factors in life that twist and turn its course. You may choose a course of action, but never realize the goal due to factors beyond your control. If you are a mature person, you understand all this, do your work, leave the rest to God, and live in peace.

Do your work, but realize that you may not be able to complete the work to your fullest satisfaction. It doesn't matter. The Bible says, "It is for you to start and for God to complete." No activity or work can be undertaken without desire or expectation. But, where there is expectation, there is frustration, too! A wise person does his work mentally prepared for any outcome. We can anticipate, at the most, only two outcomes – success or failure. If your efforts are a success, then thank God; if they are a failure, then accept it as the will of God. With that attitude you will be able to improve upon your successes and learn from your failures. *Karma yoga* is the ability to absorb the shock of failure and the excitement of success without getting overwhelmed.

When Sri Rama was offered the crown he remained calm and poised. Everyone else became excited – Sita, Lakshmana, and Dasaratha became very much excited. The only person who remained calm was Rama himself. On the following day, unexpectedly, when he was banished to the forest, he did not get upset either. Rama saw an opportunity in that calamity.

Karma yoga means keeping your mind in balance through success and failure – non-reaction to the fruits of your work. When success comes your way how do you react? You become arrogant and boast, "I am the best; look what I have accomplished!" Conversely, when depressed by failure, you wail, "*I* am a total failure." Non-reaction means doing your work and not reacting to the outcome. People misunderstand the scriptural statement that says, "You have no right over the results of your work." You think, "Krishna is speaking like an old capitalist," when he counsels you not to insist upon remuneration. However, Krishna is referring to a state of mind that is not dependent upon reward! How do you react when an expected result doesn't come? Can you keep your mind in balance in both success and failure? Doing so becomes a valuable learning experience. But if you fail to learn non-reaction, a simple success is enough for your head to swell up, and a simple failure is enough to give you a heart attack!

I was told a story about a person who had a mild heart attack. He purchased a lottery ticket, hit the jackpot and won the first prize – 50 lakhs rupees. Big money! A telegram came announcing the news, landing in the hands of his wife. When she read the telegram he was overjoyed! Now, she thought, "If I tell this news to my sband, he may get excited, collapse and die!" Not that she bothered ut his heart condition, but then, she thought, "Who will sign the se document?" So, she sought to keep him alive! But she couldn't how to communicate this good news to him, until she thought uld take the help of his psychiatrist! The doctor came and n this information piecemeal: "Sir, how are you? Suppose if you 10,000 rupees, how would you feel?" The man replied, "Well, 10,000 rupees is nothing; if I go to a five-star hotel with my friend, I can finish that amount in no time." The doctor continued, "What if you were to get 10 lakhs rupees?" The man replied, "These days, that is also nothing." The doctor asked, "And what if you received 50 lakhs?" Then the man replied, "Now that's a substantial amount, Doctor. If you give me the information about where it's available, I'll give you a gift of three lakhs." Hearing this, the *doctor* collapsed!

Any information – good or bad – can overwhelm you, even though, like the doctor, you seem well prepared. The doctor was well prepared but became overexcited. What is required is mental stamina. The mind's *muscles* need developing so that neither success nor failure will affect it. With a balanced mind, from the platform of your success, you can achieve greater success; and from your failures you can learn how to rectify what went wrong. A steady mind converts every disaster into an opportunity for growth.

The Art of Non-Reaction

Non-reaction to the fruits of your work is called *karma yoga*. This *yoga* is an attitude towards *karma* and its results. When you work, you should accept the fact that you can only do your best, and the rest is in God's hands. This way, when results come, you will be able to accept them. This does not mean that you should resign to your plight. Your only plight is to be a realized person! A quiet and serene mind is capable of gaining that understanding. To gain a serene mind, learn the art of non-reaction.

When Krishna says, "*ma phalesu*," he is not suggesting that you should ignore thinking about the results of your actions (II:47). You are to think about the results. Otherwise, making effort and taking initiative will be inhibited. For example, when you leave from home, you have a result, a destination, already in mind. What was the result that you expected? It was to reach the lecture hall where a discourse on the *Bhagavad Gita* was being given. If someone stopped and asked you, "Where you are going?" and you answer sincerely, "I just don't know; God alone knows," you will not even be able to take one step forward. Clarity is vital to achieving your intended goal.

Different levels of clarity are vital to different situations. If you invest your money, you must know if it is secure, have some idea about the return on your investment and when to expect those returns. Do not foolishly quip, "I left everything to God!" God has given you intelligence. Use it. But once you have taken a decision after considering all the details, thereafter cease to worry about it.

Have you heard the story of the farmer who put his money in the bank? The farmer deposited some money in the bank, and, that night he couldn't sleep. He turned and tossed in his bed. Finally, he woke up his wife and convinced her that he must go to the bank to see if somebody was standing guard. When he reached the bank, to his horror, he found that no guard was anywhere near the bank. He rushed back home and told his wife, "Since nobody is near the bank, I'll go and sleep on the steps of the bank building!" Would you do such a thing? Your money is secure in a bank! With that knowledge, deposit your money and leave the bank officials to see to their duty.

The ability to free your mind from completed work so that you can turn to other duties is another dimension of *karma yoga*. Instead of continuously worrying about the decisions you have made, or the work you have done, keep moving! That is the meaning of *sannyasa*, to do your work, leave the rest to God and be happy. Quit looking back again and again. But for most of us, one achievement is enough for us to gloat over for the rest of our lives! Suppose you happen to write a poem. Then you have it printed and framed, and whoever comes to your house is obligated to read it. And if they don't appreciate it according to your expectations, you feel depressed. You vow, "I'll never write a poem again!" Whereas, once a real poet composes a poem, he never again bothers about it. He marches ahead.

Giving God His Due

When you receive the results of your work, refrain from thinking that the results are your exclusive property – *Ma karma phala hetur bhur* (II:47). For example, if a student receives a distinction in the university, is that student the exclusive of the award? The entire universe cooperated with the student – his mother who kept vigil all the while he was studying late at night, who frequently served him hot tea, gave her abiding love; his father whose income took care of the family's daily needs; the teachers who taught him; the servants who served him – not the student alone, but the entire universe cooperated! The stars placed themselves in favorable positions. An entire conspiracy of apparent coincidences occurred creating that particular result!

All that you achieve is not your personal accomplishment. It is the accomplishment of the whole cosmos. This realization makes you humble. Also understand that your achievement is shared; it is cooperative work. It is the work of Universal Intelligence, so don't make any claims of your individual success. Likewise, don't feel badly if you are not successful. Don't become the *karma phala hetur*, "the author of the result." See the Lord as the author of the poem of your life.

You may posit, "The Lord does everything, so I don't have to do anything! I will just sit and simply think of Lord and let everything unfold." When Krishna says, *Karmany ev'adhikaras te ma phalesu kadacana* – "Do your duty without attachment to the results," he did not mean you should remain idle! (II:47). Rather he means, "Do your best and then leave the rest to the Lord." If you stop doing your mite, leaving *everything* to the Lord, *nothing* will work! You must do your part, remaining ever active.

Four Principles of Work Life

These are the four principles of work:

1) You are responsible for choosing a course of action keeping a worthy goal in mind;
2) Be balanced in your assessment and response to the outcome of your efforts;
3) See your work as a channel of Cosmic purpose; and,
4) Remain dynamically active in this interactive world of work.

When you carry out your mundane activities, you always have expectations. Others may not appreciate your work. The world is thankless, especially when you excel in your work. No one will appreciate you. They may even turn against you. Conversely, if you are in trouble, people may sympathize with you, getting vicarious satisfaction from your misfortune. If you do well, people may become jealous. You complain, "Nobody appreciates me!" Craving for appreciation makes you disappointed. As a result, you cease to enjoy work. Hence, the general tendency among people to finish their work quickly and move onto pleasure-seeking activities, or, if possible, evade work entirely. We might even make somebody else do our job and then pretend that we did it. We just do not enjoy what we are doing. All because we are craving for outside recognition!

Work is Worship

Krishna says that it is important that you enjoy what you are doing.

When you understand the principles of the cause and consequences, you will be able to enjoy what you are doing. *Karma yoga* is enjoying one's work and not reacting to its outcome. When you practise *karma yoga* any work becomes enjoyable to you. You can do any work – scrub the floor, be a scavenger, become a philosopher, be a professor, be a plumber – any work you will enjoy. It is not the work or the nature of the work, but the *attitude* with which we do the work that is important. With the right attitude, work becomes an offering and worship.

There is a beautiful saying uttered by Mahatma Gandhi: "Work is worship." Gandhi elaborated upon this idea when he said, "Worship without sacrifice is meaningless." We work and worship, but we do not necessarily integrate work with worship. We worship the country, but we do nothing for the country. Worship we do – in the temples or in our *puja* room at home – but without true sacrifice. What exactly is the meaning of worship? Worship means sacrifice, something that you give. What is that which you can give to God? Maybe, you can give a flower – plucked from your neighbour's garden; or maybe a fruit – that, too, rotten. Perhaps some of the fruit that you bought turned out to be rotten, then you thought of God: "God, this is for you!"

Authentic Sacrifice

There are different ways of worshipping God – *namaskara* (prostrations); *bali* (offering a fruit); or, *stuti* (glorification) – but do you think that God *requires* your glorification or that he will *feel* glorified? Who feels praised? A person who has no respect for himself will feel praised. If you have no respect for yourself, you will feel praised by praise, because inwardly you are empty. If you know who you are, if you have respect for yourself, you cannot feel elated at being praised by anybody. Whenever you feel praised, you open yourself up for exploitation and start dancing according to the wishes of others who praise you.

Can God be glorified by your praises? No! Then, what is authentic sacrifice? What sacrifice can you make for God? The only authentic sacrifice you can make for God is your work!

Your work is the best offering to God. The *Gita* says,

> *Yatah pravrttir bhutanam yena sarvam idam tatam*
> *sva-karmana tam abhyarcya siddhim vindati manavah*

"Worship God through your work for final fulfillment" (XVIII:46). Conscientious and diligent performance of your work becomes the greatest offering to God, because that alone is your unique contribution. What, other than your work, can you give to God? All other offerings are mere tokens.

What is work? Work is what you do in a relationship, what you bring out in relationship. It can be a physical work; it can be a word; it can be a gesture; it can be a look. When you are in a relationship, something is invoked. What is invoked in a relationship through your sense organs, your body, your mind, your intellect is called work. Work is to be given as an offering to the Lord, but how do I make an offering to an invisible God? Everything extant is a modification of *Brahman*, the creation of the Lord. So, if I give a cup of tea to you, I am giving it to God *through* you. The awareness gradually comes to you that invisible laws govern the world. Furthermore, there is a Law Giver, an Intelligent Principle behind the world and all its manifest forms. Taking up this frame of mind is how we gradually come to the awareness of God.

The Concept of God

Nietzsche said that God is dead; somebody else said that God is alive. How do you understand the concept of God? You continuously interact with the world around you. The universe enters into you and you enter into the universe that is operating according to laws. Any law must have an intelligence supporting it. God is the intelligent Law Giver. One definition of God is that he is Cosmic Intelligence, the principle that maintains the entire complex universe. When you offer your work to that Lord, that offering becomes worship. When you touch your parents' feet, you are touching the Lord's feet through them. You feed God when you feed a poor beggar.

With this attitude you develop a vision that transcends specifics, opposites and contradictions – a vision by which you can see the principle that holds the entire web of existence within its intelligence. Your spiritual sensitivity awakens. Once work becomes worship and an offering, you can never be bored. Work will be an ecstatic experience because you offer your work to that higher Principle, to Him whom you worship and love, and who is great. When you do a work for a great person, don't you feel excited? Why is it so? It is because you are excited about that person, love that person, care for that person. Once you have respect for God, all your work becomes an offering to Him. You will happily do any work – sweeping the streets, making a meal, working in the factory, driving a car or managing your office – whatever job that God has assigned to you. You will realize that he is the Director and that you are only playing a role in His cosmic drama. Read your script and play your role with this vision. God has given the script telling you how to conduct yourself in this world. Krishna says,

Sa ev'ayam maya te' dya yogah proktah puratanah
bhakto'si me sakha c'eti rahasyam hy etad uttamam

"I have taught this in the Vedas, in the religious books of the world. From good and wise people you learn how to play your role and how to enjoy life" (*Gita* IV.3).

When you can convert your work from boredom to an experience of ecstasy, you will be able to apply yourself to any kind of work. When you do your work happily, happiness is multiplied. Work will no more be work for you. At the end of Krishna's discourse on *karma yoga*, Arjuna suddenly discovers his role in the world – in the whole scheme of things – and realizes that he is doing God's work. When you do your work as God's work, then God does your work. This is the greatest ecstasy. Your vision becomes part of the Total Vision, the macrovision. To the extent that our personal work resonates with the Cosmic Will, to that extent we are successful.

Five

The Many Faces of God

SARVADHARMA SAMABHAVANA

There is no kingdom without an army,
no army without wealth,
no wealth without material prosperity,
no material prosperity without justice,
no justice without God.

A Pre-Islamic Sasanian Saying

Karma Yoga is renouncing reaction, a discipline of doing work as worship and receiving the fruits of work as a gift from God, the Master of all Works. Reactions emanate from distilled memories with a predictable pattern of manifestation. Restraint of reaction leads to clarity of mind and to spontaneous right action.

Programme of Self-Unfoldment

To begin with, reaction has to be deliberately restrained. Such a conscious practice of restraining reactions is called a *sadhana*. It is like turning the flow of a river to the direction of its source. The *sadhaka* values non-reaction, though in practice he often fails. Only an assimilated value matrix inspires character and conduct.

Reaction can be counterbalanced by deliberation. It is a painful exercise, but adequate efforts, reinforced by a prayerful disposition, empowers the seeker to organize his psychic energies into positive channels. Krishna says,

> *Yam hi na vyathayanty ete purusam purus'arsabha*
> *sama-duhkha-sukham dhiram so'mrtatvaya kalpate*

"He who is not swayed by pain and pleasure, verily, that steady-minded person accesses the power of the immortal Self" (*Gita* II.15). This is the programme of self-unfoldment the *Bhagavad Gita* presents.

Reducing the Doer-Enjoyer Gap

People are not happy in work. They think that happiness is in the possession and enjoyment of the fruits of their work. Worldly people work with expectation, but, alas, such projects invariably end up in failure. They become disappointed.

It is like shopping, which is an addiction these days. You compulsively visit shop after shop only to later toss your purchases into oblivion, into the back of your closet. Even when your desires are fulfilled, there is no real fulfillment. The gap between the doer-worker and the enjoyer-consumer remains to torment the individual. An unhappy doer cannot be a happy consumer.

The unhappy worker continues to be unhappy even when he attains an expected reward. Whipped by his discontent, the unhappy person continues to work, hoping against hope, seeking contentment elsewhere. Thus moving from one unhappiness to another his miseries remain unmitigated. It is this gap between the doer and the enjoyer that is the breeding ground of misery. You can never become happy until this gap is reduced and eventually closed.

Work is to be enjoyed. That is the only lasting enjoyment one can possibly have – the joy of flowing with work. As you work with this attitude you find happiness within. Work enjoyed is leisure. Leisurely work leads to comprehensive success. As you enjoy work the gap closes and happiness is experienced as your innate nature.

To close this gap one begins with non-reaction. You don't allow the nature or outcome of work to colour your self-perception. The environment cannot defile or define you. Practice of non-reaction, that is the use of appropriate response or pro-action, is the *sadhana* recommended for mastery of the environment. You might want to shoot your tormentor, instead, give him a flower. The instrumental value of non-reaction – of appropriate response – is the only route to Self and self-unfoldment.

As you practise these values they become your nature. Thereafter, you never lose your temper. You are incapable of anger. You laugh away all your negativities. That power to laugh away all our imaginary fears and anxieties is the highest spiritual achievement. Mind becomes quiet and the understanding that "I am not the doer," dawns upon you.

Why do we cling to our sense of doer-ship? Because of our attachment to the result! We want to possess, control and enjoy the outcome of work. We keep a list of our sacrifices, deeds and investments. Everyday we check the balance sheet of life's gains and losses.

You are Only an Instrument

He who is not worried about the outcome of his effort gains peace of mind. He knows that the maturation of work follows objective laws of causation that are beyond human control. With this understanding, one realizes that he is not even the doer, but only an instrument in the Divine Hand. Mother Theresa once said, "I am only a pencil in the Hands of God. He uses me to scribble the poem of my life." The Mother knew that she was not the author of her life, but only an instrument in the hand of her Creator.

The instrument is powerless. The body-mind complex and the neural-networks are mere trash. What is the value of such equipment? Someone said that it costs only two dollars to buy all the minerals that constitute the body. But once the body-mind becomes dynamic, infused with the spark of life, great ideas and profound deeds are accomplished.

When you dis-identify with the body the hidden power that expresses through the mind is realized. It is commonly understood, when we see a glowing bulb radiating light, that the light is not the bulb. It is electricity, a power other than the bulb expressing through the tungsten wire. Those who have any doubt about the existence of invisible electricity may remove the bulb and put their finger into the socket and get shocked into the realization of electricity! Similarly, realize that there is a higher power expressing through you, enabling you to walk, to speak, to hold, to feel, to think.

As your attention turns to the Higher, the doer-enjoyer gap closes and fuses into the unfoldment of natural bliss. You recognize God as the sole author and owner of all creatures, including you. There is no more claim of ownership, of even the new house that you built with your hard-earned money. Your attitude becomes, "By God's grace, I built this house – it is His abode. I am only His housekeeper." Your vision is imbued with the Spirit of God.

Introducing God

Sri Krishna says,

> *Ye yatha mam prapadyante tams tath'aiva bhajamy aham*
> *mama vartm'anuvartante manusyah Partha sarvasah*

"As people approach me, so do I reveal to them. All are, in their different ways, searching for Me. All paths lead to Me" (*Gita* IV.11).

God being Infinite Consciousness, Love, Happiness, and Beauty, can be worshipped in manifold ways and in manifold forms for different purposes and in a rainbow of moods to suit a variety of dispositions. Since God has no given form He is free to assume any form for the devotee's sake. In fact, all forms in creation are His forms. Just as the water from the ocean takes on the colour and the shape of the glassware used to carry it, so, too, God's revelation depends upon the mindset of the devotee, his or her cultural conditioning and mental training.

Discrete traditions conceive of God differently. According to these projections of Divinity, they have developed their own distinct paths – canons, rituals, hymns and theologies – to relate and communicate with God. Hinduism – being the only continuous civilization extant in the modern world – in its history spanning five millennia has, to its credit, conceived of, incorporated and embraced most of these representations of the Absolute. Consequently, modern Hinduism has great breadth and tolerance for the manifold faces of God. God, is not limited and may be conceived of in many ways

Hindus have named the unnamable, transcendental, invisible aspect of God as *Brahman* – *Satchidananda* – that is, Eternal Consciousness Bliss: the non-dual indivisible, timeless source of everything.

For the Hindu, the dynamic manifest aspect of God is *Isvara* – what Christians call Creator – omniscient, omnipotent and omnipresent; He is the Creator of the world of names and forms; He is the law-giver and the law-enforcer; He rewards and punishes creatures according to their deeds and motives.

Hindus also worship God as *Visvarupa*, an ensemble of all forms: He is the totality of manifested beings, sentient and insentient – the Cosmic Person with hands and legs everywhere, seeing through all eyes, hearing through all ears, and eating through all mouths.

Further, God appears as a special manifestation to bless humankind, to set the stalled wheel of *dharma* into motion, to protect the good and thwart the wicked. Hindus call this form of the Absolute, *Avatara*, Divine Incarnation – a Rama, Krishna, Buddha, Jesus, Mohammed, or Moses.

Subjectively, God has been conceived of as the Light of Consciousness, the Light in the Soul, the Knower-Experiencer in every living being, that which shoots through the mind-sense organ apparatus, receiving and responding to stimuli. As such, He is the Witness, the *saksi*, of inner thoughts and feelings, the *atmaprakasa* or *pratyagatma* – the subjective consciousness.

In the ritualistic religious tradition, God is seen as a spiritually invested image – a *murti* or *vigraha* – that, through a process of potent rituals and visualization, invokes His presence or represents His power. These images are meant for easing worship, meditation, inspiration and comprehension. They are also called temple images – *puja murti or arcavatara* – as in the case of *Tirupati Venketesvara, Ma Vaishnov Devi, Kasi Visvanatha*.

We can also conceive of God as the extraordinary manifestation of power (*vibhuti*) and glory, like *Indra*, *Varuna*, *Mitra*, *Aryama* and such Vedic gods invoked in the fire-sacrifice; or the *Pauranic* gods like *Hanuman*, *Nandi*, *Garuda*, *Asvastha*, *Tulsi*, *Ganga*, etc., invoked through simple rituals and penances.

The major world religions hold one or another of the above conceptions of God as an *a priori* basis for their metaphysics, theology and value system. In Hinduism we find an amalgam of these concepts, both in the popular imagination and in the scholarly disquisitions on God. The Semitic religions, Judaism and Islam, emphasize the transcendental or invisible aspect of God. But we also find their God speaking or revealing His intentions to chosen followers or incarnations, like a Moses or a Mohammed. Classic Christianity adopts a mishmash of the above formulations of God in its theology and, consequently, their ritualistic and liturgical forms of worship.

Need Fulfillment and *Dharma*

If God can be invoked in a variety of forms and be conceived in a hierarchy of concepts and values, He can also be propitiated for fulfillment of legitimate human aspirations. In fact, success in any endeavour is a result of human effort blessed by God's grace. The following are legitimate human needs for which God's intervention can be sought:

1) For progeny, wealth, victory, fame and comforts here and in the Hereafter;
2) for relief from physical and mental afflictions, from financial troubles and fear of enemies;
3) for psychic powers, namely *anima* (tininess), *mahima* (vastness), *laghima* (weightlessness), *garima* (ponderousness), *isitvam* (lordship), *vasitvam* (self-control or attractiveness), *prapti* (bi-location; flying), and *prakamya* (instant fulfillment);
4) for mental purity, maturity, and the power of non-reaction;

5) for the well-being of the world (*lokasamgraha*), for spiritual liberation (*moksa*), union with God (*sayujya*), for unconditional love (*paramaprema*).

The first two levels of need fulfillment are for physical accomplishments, the third is for mental accomplishments, and the last two are for spiritual attainment.

While the Vedas mention ritual and incantations to propitiate gods for the fulfillment of natural human needs – like progeny, wealth, victory, health, fame and heaven – the Puranas encourage a life of loving service and constant glorification of the Lord by diligent performance of daily duties. The Upanishads and other ascetic traditions teach the path of self-discipline and self-inquiry for release from material bondage. Certain *yogis* seek psychic powers to control nature and free the spirit from the limitations of matter – of hunger and thirst, and death and damnation. The Christian seeks salvation through Christ, while the Vaishnavas seek liberation through Krishna and Rama. The Buddhists seek dissolution through contemplation upon No-Thing-ness. All of them reach the same goal. You can reach the mountain peak from the east or west, from north or south, or even land on top in a helicopter. As many people, so many paths, so many descriptions – but the final experience of beauty and felicity is the same.

To illustrate this point, there is a story: Two devotees worshipped Krishna in a famous Krishna temple in Kerala. One was very rich and suffered from acute arthritis. He could not walk even a single step. The other was a young man praying to the Lord for financial assistance for his upcoming marriage. Both of them sat in the same corner praying ardently – one for a cure and the other for lucre! Then the Lord appeared to the young man in a vision and directed him, "Snatch that moneybag from the rich devotee sitting next to you! Then run as fast as you can!" The arthritic man was lost in divine ecstasy, chanting the name of the Lord. So, the young man, following the Lord's commandment, snatched the purse and swiftly ran away. Shocked out of his ecstatic mood, the sickly man abruptly halted his chanting and ran behind the young man yelling, "Thief, thief! Stop that boy!" Finally, he overtook the groom-to-be, overpowering him. As he shook him in rage and with disbelief looked into the young man's eyes, he suddenly saw his beloved Lord Krishna, smiling and saying, "O how you ran; you are cured!" Hearing this the old man fell at the young man's feet with the consoling realization that his arthritic days were over. He gladly handed over the moneybag, and the young man walked away laughing – now he could arrange his marriage!

Who Worships God?

Krishna says,

> *Catur-vidha bhajante mam janah sukrtino'rjuna*
> *arto jijnasur arth'arthi jnani ca Bharata'rsabha*

"These noble souls come to me for various reasons – one for relief from suffering and loss, another for material gain, a third for the love of knowledge, and, lastly, those who seek Me as the only refuge" (*Gita* VII.16).

The Puranas give elaborate descriptions of people in distress seeking God's intervention – i.e. Draupadi, the Pandavas' queen, molested by Dussasana, the evil Kaurava prince, in the open assembly chamber of Duryodhana and in the presence of her five chained husbands and helpless senior law-makers, like Bhishma and Drona. She cried for God's help, and help came instantly! Her royal robes outlasted the bewildered villain's attempts to disrobe her until he gave up in utter exhaustion. God *does* come to our rescue when we call upon Him: Prahlada, the young son of Hiranyakasipu, the demon king, when tormented by his father's minions, sought Divine help and received instant relief through the mediation of Narasimha, the man-lion *avatara* of Lord Vishnu. Sudhama, the dirt-poor brahmin, with thirteen children to feed, obtained an audience with Krishna and was rid of his poverty overnight. Saul, on his way to Damascus, was struck by a blinding vision and turned into a servant of Jesus Christ. He became St. Paul who nurtured the infant Christian church that later became the official religion of the Roman Empire.

Some people come to God because of their passion for Truth and Knowledge. Mahatma Gandhi said, "Truth is God." He called himself a "*satyagrahi*" – a seeker of Truth. The innate humility of Saint Francis of Assisi and Saint Theresa of Avila brought the living presence of God into their lives. People take to the path of God for different reasons, and finally, in spite of their initial motives, they all come to the same benediction, total fulfillment. Once the river joins the ocean, it sheds all its limitations and becomes one with the oceanic infinitude. It is said, *nadimulam, rishimulam na prichet*, "It is futile, to inquire into the origin of a river or a rishi."

Who insists upon a ritualistic mode of worship? Does God, or do we? There is no need for a formal prayer in a heart-to-Heart communication. Just as a baby's infantile prattle is sweet music to the mother, so too is the incoherent blabber of a devotee expressing his confused thoughts endearing to God. In fact, as the devotee turns his attention to God, his thoughts become more organized and communication effective. Devotees often compose prayers extemporaneously in the invocation of Divine grace.

How to Worship God?

God can be worshipped by prostrations or with salutations, oblations and hymns – *namaskara, bali, stutibhih*. *Namaskara* is falling flat at the feet of the Lord. How do we accomplish that? Where are the feet of the All-Pervading Lord whose feet are everywhere? Prostration is falling flat on the stomach with the forehead and knees, chest and toes touching the ground. It is done, symbolically, facing the rising sun, or in the forecourt (*mandapa*) facing a temple deity, or to one's parents, elders or *gurus*. Such salutations, done in humility and sincerity, reach God. *Bali* are material offerings consisting of cooked food, fruits, flowers, milk or incense and offered to a deity as part of ritualistic worship. The *Gita* says,

> *Patram puspam phalam toyam yo me bhaktya prayacchati*
> *tad aham bhakty-upahrtam asnami prayat'atmanah*

"Whatever is offered to Me – a leaf, a flower, fruit or water – with a pure heart, I partake of that devotional offering" (IX.26).

It is said that one tulsi leaf offered by a humble devotee is dearer to God than a ton of gold offered by an arrogant worshipper. Lord Rama ate, with relish, all the banana skins offered by Sabari, the outcast woman devotee, who in her excitement of Rama's visit to her humble hut, gave him the skin instead the fruit. Love absolves the lover of all imperfections, and the lover lives in transcendental union with the Beloved.

A third way of invoking God's grace is by glorifying Him. A hymn (*stuti*) extols God as the Creator, Protector and Redeemer of the world. The devotee remembers the Lord as the power behind all his actions and all that happens in his life. He sees the Lord as *karmadhyaksha* – Master of all Works – and as *karma phaladata* – Giver of the Wages of One's Work. The devotee undertakes all his work as an offering to the Lord, saying, *Krishna'rpanamastu!* – "This work is offered to Krishna." He accepts the fruits of his work as *Krishnaprasada* – blessings from Lord Krishna or as the divine will of God. *Stuti* means glorifying God throughout life, in success and failure, in illness and health, through the smooth and rough terrain of life, through all its ups and downs.

God accepts any offering a loving devotee makes. It is not the object offered but the attitude with which the offering is made to the Lord that makes a difference. Fixed modes of worship offered by traditional devotees – like the *pancayatana puja*, worshipping the Lord with five items, and the *shodasopacara puja*, worshipping the

Lord in sixteen steps, or the elaborate Christian masses or services – are culturally conditioned and institutionalized practices that have no binding on a true devotee. The devotee worships God anywhere, anytime, gives any offering and relates to the Lord in any manner that suits his disposition. Worship is a private affair between the devotee and his Beloved Lord.

Personal Equations with God

A variety of human emotions can be harnessed to establish personal and fulfilling relationships with God. Accordingly, the devotee may look upon God as a beloved – as Radha's feelings towards Krishna or how Sufi saints look upon Allah; a husband – as Rama to Sita; a child – like Yasoda to Krishna or Mary to Jesus; a playmate – as the cowherd women of Vrindavan related to the teenage Krishna; a brother – as Lakshmana and Rama; a Father – as Christ perceived his relationship to God in Heaven; a Mother – how *sakteyas* see God; a friend – like Arjuna beheld Krishna; a *Guru* – as Dharmaputra's vision of Krishna; a Supreme Lord – as Bhishma and Uddava perceived Krishna: a Benefactor – how Dhruva and Prahlada thought of Vishnu, and how Sudhama saw Krishna; a Master – like Hanuman's relationship with Rama; a philosopher, guide and friend – as Draupadi's experience of Krishna; a troubleshooter – like Kunti viewed Krishna; and, a rival – how Kamsa looked upon Krishna, and Ravana upon Rama.

A devotee goes through a rainbow of such relational moods in his spiritual pilgrimage. We may choose to cultivate some of these dispositions or a combination of them in establishing our personal relationship with God. For example, the gopis of Vrindavan invoked God as a playmate. They danced with him on the banks of the Jamuna in the moonlit night, to the tune of Krishna's mellifluous flute, teasing the Lord and making merry with him. Radha looked upon God as her sole Beloved. Kamsa and Ravana connected to the Lord belligerently. They also received the blessings of God and realized the supreme glory of the Divine, gaining absolute union with the Lord. As the devotee directs all his moods to the Lord, he comes to live in constant touch with God. All that happens in life is accepted as God's will – waking, you think of God; dreaming, you dream of God; sleeping, you sleep in His embrace. Your life spins around the Supreme Power who superintends the universe.

You are a part of God's creation and very special. A ripple in you causes a storm in the Ocean of Consciousness. Do your work as an instrument of God's purpose and accept the inevitable happenings of life as His gift. Remember: you are a living leaf on the tree of God.

Image Worship

To help the mind grasp ideas and ideals we use symbols – as a national flag to represent a nation and its ideals or as a company logo to project an organization's image and mission. The mind understands images. Sense organs appreciate forms and colors. The intellect comprehends causal relationship. Ego hungers for identification with something higher and more powerful, yearning to free itself from isolation, fear and insecurity. An image of God, the rituals that relate to that image, and a scripture describing the value and glories that the image represents, are all part of religious worship.

Some worship an image of God in stone, metal, clay or wood. Others worship a book, a corpse, an institution, or an ideal of world redemption through mass conversions and proclamations of an exclusive faith. For the Christian, God is the person of Jesus Christ and His sacrifice. For a Muslim God is the *Koran*, His direct and final word. For a Buddhist absolute Truth is found in the life and light of Buddha. All these formulations reflect human nature and our way of understanding the most difficult concept – by extrapolating the unknown from the known.

Although the Hindu is an image worshipper, he does not confuse the image for God, nor is he worshipping God as the image. He worships God in the image, represented by the image. The image he worships is *soaked* in God.

When the Hindu buys a stone image from a sculptor and transports it in the back of his car – packed in straw tied with ropes – he has no illusion that he is transporting God. He looks upon the image as God only after it is installed with the appropriate rituals and invested with *bhavana*, superimposing his vision of God upon the idol. Then it becomes a living deity for him. He gives a daily bath to the deity, new clothes, food, salutations, and such courtesies one would extend to an emperor or a master. He offers the deity, that he reverently installed in his home, the best produce from his farm and salutes

Him daily, seeking His blessings – especially when he leaves home on important missions or errands. And he doesn't forget to thank Him for the successful completion of the mission. Thus the image, one's personal God, becomes the centre of life, the family guardian and protector. You converse with the Lord as you would with a confidant when you are in difficulties. The image becomes a *virtual* God, and your life starts flowing in the direction of the Divine. For you, God is a daily, living reality. Thus, for the devotee, image worship is the language with which he is comfortable. And he continues to speak that language, especially in times of deep, personal crisis.

Further, you may listen to scriptures, glorifying God, and come to know that the Lord you worship in your *puja* room is the Lord of the Universe, the omniscient Creator of the world, the Light of Consciousness in your heart, and the Infinite Information that manifests as the world. Like the baby who enjoys holding his grandmother's little finger, dragging her all around, and later, when he's grown up, realizes – to his mirth and wonder – that it was Queen Victoria who condescended to be the prisoner of his infant love.

The Highest Conception of God

In Vedanta, the highest conception of God is *Brahman*. Derived from the root "brh," *Brahman* literally means "to expand; bigger than the biggest." The word *Brahman* is indicative rather than definitive; it indicates the supreme power of unqualified bigness, all-encompassing transcendence. If one takes the first meaning of the root, "to expand," *Brahman* denotes a power that expands as the Cosmos of names and forms, and then contracts into a singularity, recouping for further expansion. *Brahman* is an expanding and contracting energy.

How can one realize Brahman, the pure source of all potentiality? *Brahman* is neither realized through the senses nor by logic, nor through science and technology, but through a detached non-judgmental mind, a pure heart saturated in love. The material and mental phenomenon of the universe is a manifestation of that invisible and inexhaustible *Brahman*. It is not a static, stony *Brahman* but a dynamically manifesting symphony of beauty, the source of all mirth. Brahman is fun. *Brahman* is transcendental Truth, Immanent Consciousness, and the grand Ground of all Plurality, the Thread that integrates all hierarchies.

Sarv'edriya-gun'abhasam sarv'endriya vivarjitam
asaktam sarva-bhrc c'aiva nirgunam guna-bhoktr ca

"Functioning through the limited *upadhis* (instruments), He remains unlimited; though the ground of all, He is detached from all. He is the enjoyer of all, but corrupted by none" (*Gita* XIII.14).

What is the material from which Brahman created the world? The world that you and I experience cannot possibly come from nothing. Therefore, *Brahman* is both the material and efficient cause of creation: "*Abhinna nimitta upadana karanam*." As the material cause *Brahman* is every cell in our body, every thought in our mind, and every particle of the material universe. *Brahman* in its creative enterprise is known as *Isvara*.

One Web of Life

Finally, the devotee comes to the realization that *Brahman*, *Isvara*, is the Light of Consciousness, his deepest being, his soul and the life that throbs in all manifestation, holding the entire existence in a web of love.

God is the *ground* of all, is *in* all, *is* all, and is *beyond* all. He is me, you, this and that! Thou art That!

Six

Laws of Karma

KARMASIDDHANTA

Those who continue to work hard on right lines
and without any decline in commitment
will vanquish even fate.
Thiruvalluvar-Kural

A Multidimensional Approach to God

We were trying to understand the concept and experience of God in the last chapter: how a global person, under the influence of multicultural values, under different kinds of pressures understands the concept of God. How does a person who is exposed to different wisdom traditions of the world look at God?

We have taken a multidimensional approach to God, that you can reach God though coming from different directions. Our experience of God is very rich. There is not even a single moment of time, nor any activity where God is removed from us. We have brought God into the centre of our lives, into our feelings, into our cognitions, into our experiences. We have made Him a participant in our worldly activities. We understand God as the Ultimate Field of all Possibilities, as the Blissful Awareness and Consciousness, as the Organizing Principle integrating all manifestations in the universe, as the Power which maintains the harmony and rhythm of the world, causes the flow of energy in creation, as the Indwelling Principle which makes us function and gives us the feeling of health and well being, as your individual consciousness. That is the way we understand the nature of God.

God is a very profound phenomenon to be experienced, not just an idea to be conceptualized. God can be represented variously. He is the sacrificial fire into which you offer your oblation. God is worshipped as the Sun, the Lord of our universe whose light gives life. The incarnations and representations of God are many. He can be invoked for the fulfillment of your legitimate desires. The *Gita* says, *Dharm'aviruddho bhutesu kamo'smi Bharta'rsabha* – "I am desire that is unopposed to *dharma*" (VII.11). You may propitiate God when your desire is legitimate, when your desire is not hurtful to your neighbours. Thereby, God becomes a participant, a partner in your life – like Rama became a partner to Sugriva, and Krishna a partner to Arjuna. God becomes ubiquitous in our lives.

You can approach God for the fulfillment of your legitimate desires. You can propitiate God in various simple and humble ways: by prostration, *namaskara*, offering a flower or even a drop of water. You need not overspend to propitiate God! One's relationship with God is a matter of attitude.

From this standpoint, there is nothing to argue about God. We don't have to move away from the world to meet God. You can be in the world, in the midst of all religions and cultures, and still experience God. That was the experience of Ramakrishna who reached God through Christianity, through Islam, and through Hinduism. Ramakrishna's experiment of finding Truth in every religious tradition exemplifies a multidimensional approach to God. A multidimensional approach is what Vedanta prescribes and what the modern man wants – a God in whose name we need not fight, a God with whom we enjoy partnership for the fulfillment of our genuine desires, and for *moksa*, ultimate freedom.

Moksa can be understood in various ways. It can be nearness to God. It can be unfolding your potential. It can be living in the total freedom of spontaneous right choice. It can be living in unconditional happiness and love.

The Problem of Suffering

Even though we have all these explanations of God, the experience of suffering remains. Pain and suffering are existential conditions of human life. There are four predominant metaphysical positions that we can take when dealing with the problem of suffering:

1) everything is *Brahman*:
2) everything is *sunya*;
3) everything is God's creation; and
4) everything is due to *karma*.

However, suffering and pain cannot be eliminated with mere theoretical understanding. You cannot explain away pain.

Of these four philosophical views, the Vedantic position is that everything is *Brahman*: *Sarvam khalvidam brahma*. "There is nothing other than *Brahman*." *Brahman* is pure bliss. And you are that *Brahman*. Therefore you also should be pure bliss. But even if I explain this position to you and you become convinced, your suffering still remains. Your suffering is not an intellectual conclusion – it is an experiential fact. When a thorn goes into your flesh, you may draw the intellectual conclusion that you have no pain – that you are *Brahman* – but your suffering will continue. The intellectual conclusion that everything is *Brahman* does not explain away your problem of pain and suffering.

A second position is that of the Buddhists. They say that everything is *sunya*. "Pain is emptiness," they say, but even if you take this position, your problem of suffering remains. Theoretically you may agree to this and meditate upon *sunya*, but when a mosquito lands on your nose, you cannot resist the temptation of swiping it away. The Buddhist position that everything is *sunya* also does not help you to relieve your suffering.

A third position is of the *Isvaravadi*, the theist – that everything is

God's creation. The Creator is compassionate, all-knowing and all-powerful. But then, we wonder, how can the all-knowing, all-compassionate God create suffering? We are painfully born through suffering into suffering. Everything is painful. Everything is *duhkha*, as Buddha said. Why should an all-powerful, all-knowing, all-compassionate God create suffering? This spontaneous and natural question arises from our observations and experience. We may respond, "Well, then, such a God cannot be *all that* powerful," taking the why-bad-things-happen-to-good-people approach. Or you may conclude that another power other than God – like Satan – created suffering. God tries to eliminate suffering, but Satan seems to be more successful.

How can an all-powerful, all knowing, all-compassionate God create suffering? This question bothers people who *think*, people who *are* compassionate. There is an explanatory gap between your experience of suffering and the explanations that are offered. You experience pain. You have fear. You don't want to be old. If you were granted an option between youth and old age, which one would you choose? If choice were possible we would chose to remain youthful, to be vigorously healthy, and to avoid the painful process of dying. If we probe into our secret thoughts, none of us want to grow old; none of us want to be sick; none of us want to die.

We seem to be helpless in understanding why there is suffering. What is suffering? Suffering means going through the ordeals brought on by old age, disease, deprivation, disrespect and death. Suffering is the central experiential fact of life that cannot be easily explained away with theories or logical conclusions. We might try to create a certain psychological or physical conditioning by which we become immune to pain and/or lessen the mental suffering that accompanies any debility. We pursue immunity from suffering and pain through *yogic* exercises, *pranayama* or through the power of positive thinking. We try to overcome suffering through hypnotic conditioning of the system. We may temporarily avoid suffering with the use of certain drugs or medications, but none of these give a permanent relief from pain.

How do we explain this situation? Since there is an explanatory gap between our philosophical explanation, our theoretical assumptions and what we undergo in life, we need a variety of explanations to help us understand and cope with human life. One explanation is insufficient. We may try to look at life from a single standpoint, but that alone fails to explain *all* our experience. That is why a fourth metaphysical explanation – the *karma* theory – is offered.

Karmasiddhanta: *Karma* and Ego

We have another way of looking at life to make some sense of our experiences. We have been looking at life from the standpoint of an omnipotent God; looking at life from the standpoint of *Brahman* – the unrelated, uncontaminated, unaffected, supreme, blissful Consciousness; and, looking at life from the standpoint of *sunya* – that everything exists in a relationship of dependent origination – the theory that any given phenomenon, being a combination of more basic phenomena, has no innate existence.

"Suffering is of the ego," we assert. "Therefore, be free from ego and suffering will cease." Try to shed your ego, and the more you try, the more egoistic you become. In various ways we try to hide behind an explanation – and, at least theoretically, put our suffering under the carpet of that explanation. Suffering is still there; we just don't acknowledge it. We don't confront it. To fill this explanatory gap, we introduce *karmasiddhanta*, the law of *karma*.

From the standpoint of the law of *karma*, the individual, as choice -maker, is a free agent. There is God, who is the Organizing Principle; there is *Brahman*, the field and source of all energy; and there is the individual, who is the choice-maker. The *Gita* says, *Karmany ev'adhikaras te* – "You have choice over your actions" (II.47). When the individual makes his choice in tune with the law of *karma* he brings out his full potential, the power of *Brahman* through action. You can bring out the power of *Brahman* – the ability as choice-maker to re-create yourself infinitely – because you are a channel of that *Brahman*. You can bring out the power of *Brahman* through your actions, through your thoughts, through your desire-fulfilling activities, provided you are able to organize your thoughts and actions in tune with the laws operating this universe – the laws of *karma*.

Being in tune with the law of *karma* is something like managing fire. How do you relate to fire? If you don't know the laws that govern fire, you run the risk of getting burnt. If you know the law of fire, you can utilize fire to your advantage. Only if you understand the law of gravity, can you utilize the law of gravity, apply your scientific acumen to create the hardware necessary to exceed gravitational force and send man to the moon! If you know a particular law, you can use it to your advantage. Similarly, if you understand the law of *karma* and how to apply that law in your daily life, in your choice-making, then you can utilize the law of *karma* to fulfill your destiny. If you misunderstand, or are unfamiliar with, the law of *karma*, you tend to make all kinds of wrong choices and cause your own suffering.

Man as Choice-Maker

It is vital that, as a free choice-maker, we know and understand the law of *karma*. We make choices moment to moment. Choice-making starts early in the morning; your first choice is whether or not you should get up. After getting up you have to make other choices – "Should I first take a cup of coffee or brush my teeth?" Finally you decide to have tea. Realize, that from moment to moment, we engage in making choices.

An animal does not have to exercise such choices. Animals act instinctively. If you stamp on the tail of a dog, the dog will leap up and bark. The dog is not making a choice; it is acting in accordance with its programming. It is programmed under certain circumstances to bark. But if somebody steps on your toe, you first check out his size. You see that he is a six-footer and you are tiny, so your first option – to punch him on the nose – is ruled out. Instead you choose to speak up and politely point out, "You stepped on my toe," so that, catching the hint, he moves his foot away.

Man is a self-conscious being. In your conscious awareness you exercise your "personal computer," toy with various options derived from past experiences. Various options are juggled around. You attempt to make appropriate choices. If you don't make the appropriate choice, later on you regret the choice you made. Then regret becomes the conditioning principle of your next choice. You think, "I won't say anything next time, even if a puny man stamps on my toe," because just yesterday that six-footer whom you encountered gave you a bloody nose! Once bitten twice shy!

Karma and Responsibility

As a choice-maker we consider our options. We have the ability to reflect upon our thoughts; we know the results that we want from particular actions that we choose to undertake; and, we have the ability to foresee consequences. When you have a desired result in mind, you modify your choice-making accordingly. The responsibility of man is to make his choices very intelligently, so that he attains the results he desires. Thus, according to the laws of *karma*, man becomes responsible for his choices.

Karmasiddhanta is not fatalism. *Karmasiddhanta* ordains you to be the master of your destiny. *Karmasiddhanta* attests that you build the palace or prison of your life brick by brick, thought by thought, according to the choices you make. If you make wrong choices, then the house you construct will be paltry and inferior. If you make the right choices, life will be happy and peaceful. *Karmasiddhanta* asks that you neither blame God nor anyone else, but that you take charge of your life. You are the choice-maker. *You* are the actor. With right choice-making, you build your life, make your destiny and become the master of your own life.

Knowledge and understanding are prerequisites for making choices. We have value systems. We have the Vedas and we have our wisdom traditions. We can fall back on those traditions as reliable sources in helping in our decision-making process. For example, our own wisdom tradition indicates that the survival of any race depends upon their ability to make the appropriate choices. Indians seem to have the right choice-making genes and are great survivors. Our spontaneous choices are generally right choices. We survive amidst remarkable disorder and make split-second decisions in unbelievable traffic. We lie without a blink, cover up our intentions by sweet words – survival skills for a colonial people. Historically we have been great survivors! Look at the world civilizations. Where is the Egyptian civilization? Where is the Sumerian civilization? Where is the Roman civilization or the Greek and Aztec civilizations? Where is the Chinese civilization? India is the only country in this world whose civilization has had continuity from the Vedic period. Even today we chant the *Gayatri mantra* that was repeated 5,000 years ago. Even today we worship fire, as did our ancestors. Our civilization has 5,000 years of continuity. We are survivors. Other civilizations died. We are thriving. We are great choice-makers. Knowing exactly what to do under different situations is how this civilization survived while others disappeared like dust under our feet.

As choice-makers we become responsible for our lives. We don't blame others. We see life as ordered by the law of *karma*. Knowing the law of *karma*, we can organize our lives to order a more fulfilling destiny. Now we must apply our understanding of the law of *karma* and make choices for a better future. We find that all old civilizations – in India and whatever still survives in China or Japan or Africa or Europe or Russia – believe in the theory of *karma*. Buddhism accepts the theory of *karma*. Confucianism believes in the theory of *karma*. Even early Christianity at one time believed in the theory of *karma* and reincarnation. The theory of *karma* is also a theory of rebirth. They go together. All over the world these two theories are again coming into prominence helping us understand the mystery of life.

American civilization, being only 300 years old, is a "child civilization." America does not know how to either explain or cope with old age, diseases and failures in life. Their understanding of the theory of *karma* and rebirth is only now coming into their awareness and inch by inch taking hold. A young, inexperienced civilization handles life's vagaries much differently than an older civilization. Haven't we all experienced failures? Most of the time we fail in our endeavours. Our successes are infrequent. We are ill most of our lives and don't know why, and then suddenly we die. Failure, illness, old age, misfortune, death – how do we explain the course of our lives? We are unable to find either causes or total remedies for these maladies.

A young civilization will address these problems materially. If you experience a midlife crisis or are suffering from the problems of old age; a child civilization recommends going to a psychiatrist. You become even more ill taking those pills that the doctor prescribed. Can you cure psychological problems – the symptoms of the lack of philosophy, religion and a wholesome worldview – by swallowing tablets? In a young civilization, psychological and philosophical problems, experiential and existential problems are thought to be curable by taking pills. That is why most of its people become crazy after some time. They think that they can solve all life problems by swallowing pills and tablets. Americans consume about 500 billion dollars' worth of sleeping pills. Still they suffer from insomnia. And in India, we sleep all the time! We should add this amount to our national GDP! It is the invisible wealth in this country.

A young civilization like America has no adequate provision for handling the existential problems of life. What will you do when you are incurably ill? What will you do when you are old, when everybody renounces you, including your children? What will you do when you are a thorough failure in life? What will you do when you are born an idiot? How do you cope with all these situations? We need an explanation for all these phenomena – why you are ill, why you suffer in spite of all that you do to prevent it.

The Inevitable Constants of Life

There are certain inevitabilities in life, constants that we have to face. I find that I am suffering, but my neighbour is not. How do we explain this? Suffering and pain are existential facts. To *integrate* suffering and pain into life is to *explain* suffering and pain. We cannot dismiss them. The theory of *karma* is offered to explain these phenomena. Suppose you are incurably ill. Your whole body is in pain. Pills don't work. You are advised not to work. That doesn't help. Your near and dear ones suggest that you chant the *Bhagavad Gita*. Religion also doesn't help you. How then do you cope with your suffering?

First understand that what you are suffering today is the result of what you have been doing in your past. What you undergo today is the result of your past choices and actions. This is the only way to explain your suffering. It can be something that you did in this life or in a previous life. Sometimes, you find children born with congenital problems. Sometimes they are born as geniuses. We explain these phenomena by tracing the cause back to something in the past, either something in this life or in a previous life. Suppose you have got a lung problem. Your lungs are weak and at the age of 35 you cannot breath. Your problem now is bronchitis. What is the cause? Your past habit of smoking brought on this condition.

Karmasiddhanta tries to explain your present situations in terms of your past choice-making. Since you chose not to study in the past, you suffer today. Since in the past you chose to smoke, today you suffer from bronchitis. Since in the past you chose to drink, you suffer today from sclerosis of the liver. When the consequences visit you, then you realize, "I shouldn't have done that!" Haven't we all gone through this type of self-flagellation, of regrets and remorse, pondering over life's ifs and buts? Whatever our parents told us – that we never followed – we start teaching to our children, thinking, "I didn't follow their advice, and I am suffering; but my children should not suffer."

Karmasiddhanta seeks to explain your present condition and experiences in terms of the previous path you undertook. The law of *karma* says that your present suffering is the consequence of your past choice-making – wise or foolish. You chose that path. You chose it deed by deed. Haven't you already chosen your present pain and suffering when you smoked the first cigarette twenty years ago? We can understand our present by looking into the past, and we may peep into our future by becoming mindful of the kind of choices we make today.

Windows of Opportunities

The space that we are living in today is full of possibilities. Though we are suffering consequences of past *karmas*, we can utilize that space to make an about turn and create a better future. *Karmasiddhanta* opens the window of opportunity. Here you are, suffering for past deeds and choices. Now is your opportunity. Understand and utilize this knowledge of *karma*.

We Indians don't have many psychological problems. We tend to explain things in terms of *karma* and *punarjanma*, rebirth. When someone abuses you, don't you think that you must have abused him in the previous birth? In America if a husband beats his wife, the following day she will take her baggage, leave and file for divorce. An Indian wife may reflect that in a previous birth her husband could have been a rat, and she may have been a cat, and that she harassed and badgered him constantly. So, in this life, she became his wife, and he is only paying her back in the same coin. This line of thought is how we carry on smoothly with life. Once the initial heat is over, the two come together again. They start talking. He regrets his actions. She says, "It doesn't matter, you must have acted under some pressure or tension." Both understand each other and, over time, change their behaviour.

We always have an opportunity to understand the connections and adjust to the life's contradictory experiences. This does not mean that you must always regress and relive the past to understand exactly what happened, nor does it mean to passively accept everything that happens. *Karmasiddhanta* provides a means by which you can understand your past by simply seeing your present circumstances.

Sometimes people come to swamis seeking to know what they were in the past. But by self-introspection, you yourself should know! By the way you think, you should know. By your compulsions and psychological complexities you should know. Of course, there are always people who will tell you that in your past life you were Queen Victoria or King Ashoka. Is there any necessity of knowing exactly what happened in the past? Your present life gives an explanation for your past – whatever you are today is the result of the choices you made in the past. You are not inferring from the past to the present – rather you are inferring from the present to the past. Thus you can explain the way things presently happen. There is no need to go to a psychiatrist. You can set aside all those tablets and pills, and you will not be driven to have a nervous breakdown.

When problems overcome you, generally you don't know what to do. You go for a couple of drinks or a smoke or you drive away to nowhere. *Karmasiddhanta* gives a peep into the past and into the future and explains why you are, *whatever* you are, and *wherever* you are, today. Understand that if you want to make a better future, you must make an effort to make right choices now.

Three Laws of *Karma*

There are three laws operating under the theory of *karma*: The first law of *karma* is that it is a process with a beginning and an end. *Karma* is not just action, but action and its consequence – the *karmaphala*, or fruit of the action. The cause and the consequence are together called *karma*. The second law is that the result, *karmaphala*, is a modification of the cause, *karma*. The third law is that all choices are intentional whether you are conscious or unconscious of your intentions; and, further, the results of karma come back to the doer – the chooser who performs the *karma*.

Karma is a release of energy, a momentum. It begins when someone chooses to initiate a *karma*. *Karma* also has an end. To understand the term *karma*, you have to see both the beginning and the end – *arambha* and *antya* – two sides of the same coin. When you initiate *karma*, it is only the beginning; *karma* creates ripples in the world, in your environment, and in your own mind – and finally it produces a result. When the result is produced, it returns to the choice-maker and the cycle of *karma* is complete.

When you smoke your first cigarette, is it over? No! Until you suffer the consequences of smoking, the *karma* is incomplete. When you abuse someone, the *karma* is not over. That someone harbours a grudge against you and one day plans to strike back. Then you wonder, "Why did *that* happen?" You should know better. You created a disturbance in the total energy field and it came back to you. *Karma* is incomplete until the results come. The beginning and the end are two sides of the karmic process. When we hear people say, "It's my *karma*," it means that they are harvesting the consequences of past deeds. Suppose that as you were walking you slipped and fell, breaking a bone. You were admitted to the hospital with a fractured leg. What explanation are you likely to give? Most likely it will be something physiological – "I must be suffering from osteoporosis, or my bones wouldn't break so easily!" or some such medical explanation. But when you are alone how do you account for your situation? You meekly admit, "It's my *karma*!" What does *karma* mean? It means that, in the past, you must have broken someone else's leg – or at least *thought* of breaking somebody's legs. That thought vibration travels around the world. Once you send a thought, it must fulfill itself. You thought of breaking somebody's legs and that thought goes around in an invisible way without fulfillment, like a ghost. Finally it catches up with you, and you break your leg – or a pencil, or the leg of your chair – depending upon the intensity of your original thought. It might have even caught someone else – that is *his karma* – but that somebody will eventually catch you!

How are you going to explain a factual experience, something that has already happened? You cannot change or hide a fact of life.

You may try to resist, but the fact remains. How will you integrate these facts into your awareness so that you avoid becoming either crazy or cynical. If you explain it as your *karma* then you will sleep well, because you have taken responsibility for your *karma*. If you blame God then you will be unable to sleep, thinking, "Why did God choose me, in particular, to torture; in what way have I failed?" If you accept your responsibility – understanding that the things which happen to you now are the results of your previous choices visiting you – then not only will you sleep better, knowing that you can change your choice-making, but you will become large-hearted and peaceful. This realization and acceptance will make you patient, forgiving and accommodative.

Karmaphala, a Modification of *Karma*

The second law of *karma* is that the result of *karma* – called the *karmaphala* – is nothing but a modification of the *karma*. A consequence is nothing but a modification of the cause. Its contours may be different but its content will be the same. Its shape, its time, its place, its color, its taste might change but the content remains the same. How does a cause modify into a consequence? A consequence is nothing but the modified cause.

For example, suppose you have a gold ring. What is that ring? The ring is nothing but a modified form of gold. You get an oak tree from the acorn. The oak tree is nothing but a manifestation, a modified form of the seed of the oak tree, the acorn. Here is an intelligent human being. What is that intelligent human being? He is nothing but a modification of food the parents had eaten. You get 23 chromosomes from the mother and another 23 chromosomes from the father. It makes a 46 chromosomal network, and from that the first cell is born. You are nothing but a modification of the food your parents have eaten and the thoughts they generated. The food that you eat is the matter, and the thought is consciousness. Consciousness riding on matter is the living and growing cell. Modified, it becomes you and me.

Your present experience – whether good or bad – is nothing but a modification of your past deeds. Hence we sometimes use the expressions like, "It's my *karma*," "It is my bad *karma*," and "It is my good *karma*." For instance, we explain our failures as bad *karma* or an unexpected success as good *karma*. Failure to get a parking spot is bad *karma*, but when you suddenly see someone pulling his car out of a nearby space, you get a glimpse of your good *karma*.

Because of our egoistic preoccupation with the result, we don't look properly and intelligently into a situation and invariably make the wrong choice. When the result is bad and unacceptable to you, how do you explain it? You explain it by saying, "Oh well, my bad *karma*." It provides a way to keep your sanity. Who will you blame for your failure? Say that you are a new person on the ballot and nobody knows you. You stand for the election and win! How to explain your success? You can understand it as your "good *karma*." *Karma* becomes an experiential factor.

How do you integrate any experience into your consciousness without getting disturbed? You need some method to cope with the situation. One choice is to become angry with everybody. Another choice is to become an alcoholic or to leave the country and settle abroad. All options are riddled with their own problems. Therefore let us put an end to the problem here itself. Accept responsibility for those things that come your way or *come* in your way – they are either your good *karma* or bad *karma*. Now you can start with a new slate.

The Intentional Choice-Maker

The third law of *karma* is that all choices are intentional, whether we are conscious or unconscious of that fact. Some choices we make unconsciously. Others are consciously made. For example, suppose that you see a person and impulsively like him. He gives you a lift, takes you to a lonely place, suddenly brandishes a weapon and demands your wallet. What happened? Initially you thought you could trust him and you liked him. You made an unconscious choice that created a conscious experience and an unacceptable consequence. But even an unconscious choice is a choice. We measure the value of a choice by the conscious experience it creates. You are responsible even for an unconscious choice because your mind always deliberates – "Should I have done this or should I have done that." Situations trigger predictable reactions from us. For example, if I look you in the eyes and say emphatically, "You're a donkey," I can predict how you will react. You'll be really angry. But if I say, "You are a very intelligent person," then your face glows with a halo shining all around it, and positive vibrations pour out of you. Your response is predictable. Situations and persons provoke predictable responses from our unconsciously made choices.

Our whole unconscious and conscious is conditioned by the past, by our positive and negative experiences. According to *karmasiddhanta*, whether our responses are Pavlovian or deliberate, we are responsible for them. We cannot just be guided by the notion, "I felt like doing it," without understanding our responsibility for our actions. Once, President Ford was giving a speech on foreign policy at an American military academy, and a few young cadets were listening. Suddenly, before the security persons could stop him, a young man got up and rushed towards the President. He gave the President a slap, went back and sat down again in his seat. The security people rushed towards the man, caught hold of him and took him away for interrogation. Naturally they asked him for an explanation. He responded, "I just felt like it." But it was a choice he made for which he had to suffer the consequences. Of course, he did get a lot of money because of the publicity that came out in newspapers and television, and the book he wrote as a consequence of his encounter with Secret Service agents. He made choices – consciously or unconsciously – and enjoyed or suffered the consequences accordingly.

All our choices are intentional. By saying a choice is intentional we mean that we expect or anticipate a certain result from our actions. The man who slapped the President may have been imagining that he was punishing the President for a boring speech. There was some intention behind his action. Since every action is intentional, the consequences of the choice come back to the *intentor* – the one who had the intention. That is the law of *karma*. There is no action without conscious or unconscious intention.

Sowing Seeds, Reaping Results

Once you undertake an action, it sets a universal law into motion. It must return to you. Your act continues to reverberate and interact variously in the environment. Finally the energy you released comes back to you and abides in you. So the choice-maker, the thinker of a particular thought, or the perpetrator of any action eventually becomes the victim of the consequence mentally and physically.

From these laws of *karma* we understand that what we sow that we reap. He who sows wind, reaps a whirlwind. He who takes up the sword, is killed by the sword. Ultimately, your intention is like a boomerang. You throw it, and it comes back to you. There is no choice-making without an intention. Therefore, it is the choice-maker alone who becomes the enjoyer-sufferer of the consequences of his choice, and nobody else.

This understanding gives us great insight into things. If you want a happy situation then broadcast happy thoughts. What you give out comes back to you. Of course the quality of any action is determined by the motive with which you undertake the action. Are your motives for your pleasure alone at the cost of everyone else? Or are your actions undertaken for the common good? Depending upon your motives and intentions an action is resolved to be good or bad, positive or negative. Definitely and ultimately the result impinges upon you, the doer. Though you may try to escape, the law of *karma* will catch you. You may try to hide, commit suicide, or destroy the other person, but finally the long arm of *karmic* law will stretch out and grab hold of you. When it catches you, then you can no longer deny your involvement.

If you apply these three laws of *karma* in your life, your suffering will find relief. If you don't apply these laws, then you suffer the consequences. By applying these laws of *karma*, you make life a better experience. But how do we go about applying these invariable laws?

Give Happiness, Receive Happiness

The first application of *karmic* law is to understand that you are responsible for your fate. Whatever you experience today, which you cannot change with any social or technological effort, is the result of your *karma*. You have to accept the responsibility for what you cannot change in spite of your efforts to change the tide of present circumstances.

The second application is to take responsibility for your present plight by taking charge of your unconscious reactions or conscious responses. You become responsible for your future, as well, with the choices you make today. Therefore, make the appropriate choices and create your destiny.

How do you choose an action? Whenever you contemplate an action, think about your intended goal – your end goal. If you want happiness, then choose happy thoughts and happiness-producing deeds. If you choose unhappy thoughts and do deeds that create unhappiness, what will you receive in return? A poisonous weed can only produce poisonous fruits. What I do to another ought to be happy deeds, actions that will create happiness in the other. Act with the understanding that whatever you give, you will get back thousand-fold. If you plant one seedling, you get a thousand seeds in return from that tree. If you want happiness, then give happiness. If you want happiness, then sow the seeds of happiness in your relationships. You are fully capable of making such a choice.

Whatever you want, give! Do you want happiness? Then give happiness. Do you want love? Then give love. Have you shared with others? Have you given love to others? Have you given unconditional love to others? Whatever you give, that you receive. It is a simple law. If you want health, entertain healthy thoughts. Don't get up every day in the morning thinking that you have a headache. If you have a headache, don't nourish it with further thoughts of a headache. By planting such thoughts in your system, you are allowing energy to vibrate accordingly. If you think, "I have a headache," then your whole energy will support that thought.

Our energy is very fluid. After all what are we? We are a dance of atoms. Like a railway station – you will always find a crowd there, but at no moment is the crowd ever the same. The crowd constantly moves, shifts, changes. A river always has water, but the water rushing by is never the same. Perhaps you have heard the aphorism, "You cannot step into the same river twice." An ensemble of atoms, a railway station, a river – all are in constant movement. So, too, is our body. At the atomic and molecular levels our body is in constant movement – atoms fly from you to your neighbour, from the trees to you, from you to the trees, to the mountains, to the stars. At every moment a particular set of atoms constitute you, but in the next moment the constituent atoms are different. You are a flow of energy. The thoughts that you entertain attract the constellation of atoms that flow in and around you in constant motion.

The kind of thoughts we entertain, the kind of deeds we do, determine the choreography of atoms dancing in and through us. The dance – your wellness or illness – depends upon the thoughts you maintain. Having the right thoughts and doing the right deeds creates happiness, health and affluence. If you want to be a rich person, consistently maintain thoughts of affluence. You gain riches only by wishing for the wealth of all. The universe is infinitely creative. It can afford universal affluence. Maybe that is why our gods are highly ornate, decorated with gold jewelry and silks in a lavish ambience. Visualize *Vaikunta*, the abode of Vishnu. What a luxurious setting! Lakshmi, the goddess of wealth, is his consort. Visualize *Svarga loka*, the abode of Indra, caparisoned white elephants, flying horses, dancers and musicians. Everything is plentiful there. See the rainforest! What a creative abundance! Watch a sunrise – what a rich display of color, power and beauty. But instead of enjoying it, we take a photograph of the sunrise, display it in the drawing room and miss its beauty altogether. The picture is nothing compared to what we have missed. Alongside nature our human creation appears pale and meagre.

I am reminded of a modern management theory, the "Win-Win Situation." *You* can win, and *everyone* can win. The law of God is not a law of poverty. The law of God is the law of abundance and affluence. Everything is plentiful so that plenitude can flow towards us – that is, if we provide the channel by entertaining thoughts of plenitude. That is what *karmasiddhanta* tells us: whatever thoughts you sow come back to you. And hence the law, "Do unto others as you would have them do unto you." If you do good for others, what comes back to you is good. This is the only way the world operates. If you want something, first you have to give. First you have to give and then take. To enjoy affluence is to share affluence. Otherwise you will squander your precious capital, like a farmer who, instead of planting his seeds, cooks them for a meal.

Be a responsible choice-maker. Make the right choices. The universe is a mirror. Understand that what you sow that you receive. Sow seeds of happiness. Give *and* receive. It does not help only to receive, or only to give. Give love to the universe and get love in abundance. Become the architect of your destiny, your future.

To Endure is to Cure

Karmasiddhanta tells us that we can refashion our future. We can create a future of affluence, success and happiness. We can partake in the dance of bliss that the universe is. But what about the past that is impinging upon you now – your present personal and social miseries? How do you tackle them? How do you cope with your present situation, facts about which it seems you can do nothing? It is your *karma*, the impact of your own past. For example, suppose that you are a five-footer. Can you do anything about it? You may wear high-heeled shoes and pretend that you are tall, but will that change the fact of your height. It's more likely to give you a backache!

So how do we cope with the absolute factors? The first rule is to understand that whatever choices you made in the past, whatever you have done in the past – consciously or unconsciously – comes to you in the form of your present experiences. Therefore, you have to endure them. Endure and pay back your debts! In any healthy economy, your credibility depends upon your paying back debts – though perhaps not in the Indian economy! In India, in fact, avoiding paying your debts is the only way to survive! You can borrow any amount of money; but don't bother to pay it back – that has been our habit and the reason for the lack of initiative and all-around poverty.

When you undergo suffering – about which you cannot do anything – you can only endure it with the consolation that you are paying back your previous debt. If you cannot cure something, then endure it! We understand through the *karma* theory that endurance is a way to purify, cleanse and pay our debt, so that we can start anew. Endure gracefully, happily and with awareness. If you don't endure your suffering happily, you will have to endure it *un*happily, creating more bad *karmas*. As choice-maker you can decide to happily endure. When you happily endure, the situation provides an education. If you readily learn from that situation, you will reduce the intensity of pain, and you will start seeing opportunity in your calamity. In any calamity, there is opportunity. The only time that Jawahar Lal Nehru, the first Prime Minister of independent India, found available to write his famous classics was when he was in the British jails! Nehru made a calamity into an opportunity!

In every bad situation we find a message *and* an opportunity. You may have to search for these, but if you cry and curse your destiny, you will fail to see both the message and the opportunity. The window of opportunity will remain shut. For example, a very active middle-aged executive, who ignored his wife, children, parents, religion and social duties for corporate success, was stricken with a heart attack at the peak of his career. When I visited him in the hospital, he confided, "Swamiji, my heart attack was a message from God, a warning that I must slow down, care for other aspects of life and avoid driving myself beyond a limit. By God's grace, I have earned enough for my children and my grandchildren. I must learn to take life easy, spend time with my family." The present calamity opened his eyes to those areas of his life that he had ignored. Opportunity awaits him.

A young man who fell under a running bus and lost both his legs, instead of cursing his destiny, took it as a challenge and became a social worker, set up his own organization working for the rehabilitation of accident victims. He became a saviour for thousands of invalids. The story of Helen Keller's heroic struggles to overcome her deficiencies and the saga of her yeoman services to those who shared her fate are written in golden letters in the annals of human history. Stephen Hawkings, who undauntedly continues his theoretical research in spite of his dysfunctional motor organs, is another glorious illustration of human ingenuity and fortitude. These are some of the instances of human accomplishment against insuperable odds. What you cannot cure, you endure. Endurance opens windows of opportunity.

Karmasiddhanta gives us one emphatic and empowering message: To re-create yourself, utilize your knowledge of this dynamic law; align with the Organizing Power of the Universe and unlock the hidden potential of *Brahman*. In moment-to-moment choice-making, the experience of transcendence awaits you.

Seven

The Spectacle of Change

MAYAVADA

He was unfathomably profound –
a genius among geniuses – who discovered,
merely by thinking about it,
that the universe was not what it seemed.
Time Magazine, On Einstein

In the previous discussion we went into detail about the law of *karma* – how those laws could be applied to enrich our lives, to live a very creative, loving, sharing life, invoking our full potential. In applying the law of *karma*, we take charge of our lives. We feel responsible. We feel proud that we ourselves fashion our destiny, living in harmony with the world and in close contact with the

Spirit. There is no Self-unfoldment without plumbing our spiritual depths. Without an interactive harmony, there is no Self-awakening.

Maya, the Magical

The concept of *maya* is an important tool of analysis for understanding the mystery of life. The word *maya* is a derivative of the Sanskrit verbal root, *ma*, which means "to measure, to limit, to give form." The entire existence is looked upon as a phenomenon arising from hierarchies of combinations. Buddhism uses a similar tool of analysis called *praditya samudpada vada* – "the theory of dependent origination." Modern physics also has an idea similar to *maya*, the "uncertainty principle," which says that energy manifests as either a particle or a wave. The difficulty for scientists lies in predicting the state in which energy exists at a given point of time. No categorical definition about energy's nature is possible.

In Vedanta the concept of *maya* is used to discuss the nature of reality. Vedanta is the highest point of Hindu thought. Vedanta calls the world *mayikam* – magical, a work of *maya*. Like a magician's magic, *maya* sets up the world of names and forms. Just as a magician uses his black tunic and magic wand, the principle of *tamas* and *rajas* is used to create the world of objects. The black tunic – *tamas* – dulls the mind, and when the wand – *rajas* – is waved, thought-waves arise. The magician uses that state of mind to make his audience perceive things (a function of *sattva*). Once the mind is dull and disturbed, it is open to suggestion and can perceive the suggested object, even non-existing things. As in the case of magic, *maya's* power of *tamas*, *rajas* and *sattva* makes us see and experience things that have no enduring value. *Aghadita ghadana padiyasi maya* – "Maya is that power that sets up deconstructable structures."

The One As Many

Maya uses the three energies of *sattva*, *rajas* and *tamas* to hoodwink us. These energies make us see, possess and hold onto things that are transient, to build philosophies and schools of thought based on these notions. The world is *mayikam* – a projection of *maya*. *Mayavi* is the Cosmic Intelligence who uses the power of *maya*. In Vedantic thought, God, the Supreme Intelligence is called "*mayavi*" – "one who possesses and uses the power of *maya* to project the world." This theory is presented with slight differences in the various *advaita* traditions. In Shaiva Siddhanta, Shiva is considered the Cosmic Intelligence and Sakti (*maya*) is the instrument that Cosmic Intelligence uses, its power. And, the world is seen as a combination or a product of the combined efforts of Sakta (Shiva) and Sakti.

The Vedas say, *Indro mayabhih pururupam iyate* – "Indra becomes manifold through *maya*." The word "Indra" means "one who is resplendent" and refers to the Universal Consciousness. That Consciousness is self-existing and therefore intelligent. Intelligence is creative potential. Hence, Indra – through his power of *maya* – becomes the many. The process of the One becoming many is called *maya*. Why is it called *maya*? Because, when the One becomes the many, it does not really become the many. Instead, the One, *without undergoing any intrinsic change, appears* as the many. The *power* of the

One to appear as the many, without giving up its original nature, is called *maya*.

For instance, you can see that the Indian actor, Amitabh Bacchan, capably plays various roles without losing his real identity. He can play the role of a coolie, a *shahanshah* (an emperor), or that of a grandfather. But when he plays those roles, *he* does not undergo any intrinsic change; he knows that he is still the *original* Bacchan. Although he presents a *false* Bacchan to the audience, he does not forget himself – who he is otherwise in life. Without forgetting himself, he is able to project different personalities and different images in various episodes and situations. By playing the role of an ordinary coolie, he does not *become* a real coolie. On the contrary, he becomes richer – his bank balance goes up with rupees sixty lakhs, of course, taken from your pocket and with your cooperation!

Mayasakti

Similarly, the great power of Consciousness, in which you are a stakeholder and shareholder, is able to project different characters, themes, episodes and scenes, without itself undergoing any intrinsic change. The power of the Cosmic Intelligence to project itself as you and me and this manifold world, without undergoing any intrinsic change, is called *mayasakti*. This world is a projection of *maya*. It is a power of *maya*. At the same time, this world does not have any independent existence. Typically, we use the word *maya* very casually, without any insight. With insight into *maya* we see that the world around us is not different from God, the Creator.

The theory of *maya* presents the idea that the Creator and the creation are inseparable. They are one, just as gold and a gold ring are one, as ocean water and its wave are one, fire and heat are one. People generally say that Sankaracharya is a *mayavadi* – that is, "one who upholds or propagates the idea of *maya* – that the world is an illusion." True, he is a *mayavadi*. But there is a derogatory sense conveyed in that usage, and the expression loses its true meaning. When *Sankaracharya* says that the world is *maya*, he is not denying the existence of the world, he is only saying that the world is non-separable from the Supreme Intelligence.

The world is alive and intelligent. The world is divine. *Purnam adah purnam idam* – "That is complete; this also is complete because this is non-separate from That" (*Isavasya Upanishad Mool Mantra*). *Mrtyoh sa mrtyum apnoti ya eha naneva pasyati* – "One who sees a separation goes from death to death" (*Katha Upanishad* II.i.10).

The description of the world as *maya* means that the world is divine or an appearance of the divine. The world is not a product of two independent categories. It is a projection of Truth, *Brahman*. That is all that is meant by the description of world as *maya*.

Subject-Object Duality

In Vedanta, 'world' is a clearly defined term. It is a *padartha* – meaning "an object (*artha*) interpreted (*pada*) by the subjective mind." The world – which means any mental or material object presented to our awareness – is indicated by words. Any sensation presented to a subject is an object. There is no experience without objects. An object and a subject together create experience. Take the case of listening. How does listening happen? The experience of listening happens when sound vibrations impact on your tympanum. When words bang on your tympanic membrane, electrical waves are created in the brain, which are called *vrttis* in Vedanta. When *vrttis* shine in consciousness you experience sound. In the case of hearing, words are the objects and you are the subject. Sounds or forms generate *vrttis* in consciousness and produce experience.

Through the five sense organs, objects flow into you, shining in your awareness, like dust particles in a beam of sunlight. That is how you are able to hear or see, feel, taste or smell. The world is something that you experience. In every experience, there is the individual subject and an external object. Without a subject and an object, the world does not exist.

According to Vedanta, there is only one Consciousness. Differences in subjective experiences are due to differences in the conditioning of individual minds. The world unfolds in terms of subject-object dynamics, which is the meaning of *maya*.

The Cause-Effect Flow

All objects are based on a cause-effect flow. Every object in the world is either a cause or an effect and, most of the time, *both* cause and effect. For example, you are a father with reference to your son. You preceded your son. You are the cause, and your son is the effect. But, are you a father all the time? Were you a father all the time? When did you become a father? Only after your marriage when you had your children. Before that you were not a father. Till then what were you? A son. You are a son with reference to your father, and a father with reference to your children. So you can simultaneously be an effect as well as the cause.

Every object in this world falls into the cause-effect chain. Objects are links in the cause-effect flow. It all depends upon the standpoint from which you observe. From the standpoint of a son you are a father, and from the standpoint of a father you are a son. So tell me, are you a father *or* a son? The answer depends upon which standpoint you take. In fact, you are both a father and a son. From a highest standpoint you are *neither* a father nor a son! This is the meaning of *maya*.

Non-duality

Everything falls in the flow of cause-effect relationships. The ultimate cause and effect is the Creator and the creation. Even the Creator and creation, according to Vedanta, fall within the law of *maya*.

The world is something that is seen; that is why it is called *loka* – *lokyate iti loka* – something that is experienced, an object of our experience. The world, being objective, has neither subjectivity nor indivisible self-identity. The world is beholden to the subjective experiencer for its manifestation and, hence, is called *maya*.

So, the world is a phenomenon that is predicated by subject-object duality. It is part of your experience. All experiences depend upon the experiencer. Therefore, experiences have a *dependent* existence. For example, say you are in an auditorium and listen to the speaker. You see him, hear him, you can shake hands with him. The speaker is part of your world. The world that you see is something that you experience. It is not only that you experience the world, but also you experience that you are the agent of experiences. You know that *you* are listening to the lecture. Not only do you experience the world, you also experience the experiencer. Both poles of the experience-experiencer paradigm are objects of your awareness and hence, depend upon Consciousness.

When you were listening to the talk, initially you saw the speaker. You were conscious of where you were sitting, of the language, etc. But slowly, as you dwell deep into the experience of listening, the speaker disappears, words disappear, terminology disappears, you yourself disappear, and what remains is one flame of ecstatic experience. Then you transcend *maya*. Both the Creator and creation, the experiencer and the experience, coalesce into one simple non-dual blissfulness experience. Wherever there is bliss, there is non-duality.

To sum up these ideas: the world falls in the paradigm of cause-effect relationships, subject-object duality, and has no self-identity, these being only empty structures interpreted by the subject. Vedanta calls these relations *maya*.

The Four States of Experience

The world of experience, of subject-object duality, falls into four levels of awareness. The first state is the waking state. In the waking state your sense organs are active; you are aware of things within (mentation) and outside (sensation). The waking state is experiencing the external world through the sense organs.

Another state is the dream world of experience. Don't you dream? If we don't dream, then we will go crazy. Madness is born of the frustration accrued due to unfulfilled desires. God has provided us with the ability to dream. All our desires cannot be fulfilled in the waking world. But in the dream world all your desires can be fulfilled. Your dream world is your own private, subjective world. The waking world is a public, objective world that follows the laws of physics. In the dream world you become a totally different person. For instance, if you are a rich man in the waking world, in the dream world you invariably become a poor man! Ask a rich man about his dreams. The rich dream that they have lost all their wealth and the poor dream that they won the lottery! The rich man's dreams incorporate his fear of poverty; the poor man's dreams incorporate his desire for riches.

The dream world is a totally different world. We spend a lot of time in dreaming. The dream world has to be incorporated into our awareness. But unfortunately we shun it thinking that dream is not real, as though the waking state is the only reality. The dream state is as real as the waking state. One-third of our life is spent in the waking state and the other two-thirds are spent sleeping, dreaming *and* daydreaming! So how can you say that dream has no reality? If the waking state is real, dream also is real. In fact, when the dream state comes, the waking state goes; and when the waking state comes, the dream state goes. Is it not true? The two states contradict each other. Objects of the dream state are not available in the waking world. Objects of the waking state are not available in the dream world. You could dream that you are quite hungry, but you cannot appease the hunger of the dreamer with sandwiches taken from the refrigerator near which he fell asleep after a heavy lunch! The dreamer cannot avail the objects of the waking world. And the waker cannot avail the objects of the dream world. The waker negates the dreamer, and the dreamer negates the waker. They are mutually contradictory.

The deep sleep state is the third world of experience – a relatively enjoyable state. Why is sleep enjoyable? You have no thoughts, no struggle or sense of time in sleep. You don't have to reach anywhere in sleep. There are no spatio-temporal limitations in sleep. In sleep, you are not conditioned by any kind of predications. Deep sleep negates both the dream and waking states. When one arises the other disappears. The presence of one of these states negates all others.

Death is the fourth state of experience. Death is like extended sleep. Like deep sleep, you have nothing to worry about in that state. In death you go into a deep corridor of unknown dimensions, and then you emerge somewhere else as some other form – depending upon what you have done in your previous birth. The absence of memory of the death experience is no proof of the absence of the experience.

We move between these four states of experience – waking, dream, sleep and death – like a fish going up and down, forward and backward in a stream. The fish can come up to the surface, swim amongst the weeds and rocks in midstream, or dive into the very depth of the flowing water. The fish can swim upstream or downstream. Likewise we move from the waking state to sleep, to dreams, to deep sleep, and to death. All these four states negate each other and depend upon the experiencer's subjective consciousness – hence, they are called *maya*.

A King or a Butterfly?

Maya is the phenomenon of moving from one experience to another. A previous state of experience is negated when a subsequent state of experience arises. I was told the dream of a king. The king, as usual, went to take a nap after his lunch. It was a little hot, and his attendants were fanning him. The room was perfumed, and in that sleep-conducive environment the king went to sleep and dreamt. He dreamt that he became a butterfly, and that children were chasing the butterfly. The butterfly flew here and there and finally hit a wall. As it hit the wall the king woke up and found himself sleeping in his bedroom. Then he had a doubt, "Was I really a butterfly or am I a king? What is the truth of these two existences?" Then the minister was called and asked to clear the king's doubt. The minister replied that the king was a butterfly in his dream state, and that he is a king in the waking state – the later being his real state. But the king could not believe this and continued to doubt whether he was a only a dream of the butterfly! If the butterfly can be a dream of the king, why can't the king be a dream of the butterfly?

This is another feature of *maya*. *Svakale satvavad bhati*. "When you experience something, the experience appears so real" (*Atma Bodha* 6). When the experience ends, realize its fleeting and false nature. At the time of experience if anyone were to refute your delusory belief, you cannot understand. When you were a teenager, so beautiful and wonderful, you were on top of the world, almost considered for stardom. Today, at ninety – with sparse hair, false teeth and shrivelled up skin – you are an apparition of your old self. If someone were to remind you of your teenage experiences, what will your reaction be? You will say, "Stop insulting me!" You don't wish to be reminded of your earlier days. Your wish is to flow with life, to continue forward. For you, experiences blossom and disappear like a flower. They bloom in the morning and they are gone by evening. What remains is a handful of haggard and dead memories that have no reality in your present life.

The Constancy of Change

The waking, dream, sleep and death states are together called *maya*. Everything is constantly changing. Our experience seems so true – while it is available. Hence, in Vedanta, it is said that when an experience is available it should be enjoyed to the maximum, since the following moment it fades. Like a drop of water in a frying pan, it just makes a little noise and then disappears. Every experience is momentary. When it is available, enjoy it, so that you will not keep a memory of it when it ceases to exist. You have to go through the experience, enjoy it to the hilt, so that when it is not available you are not craving for it, and, when it flies, you can say goodbye to it.

When an experience comes, don't resist it – *agate svagatam kuryat*. When the experience goes, give it a grand send off – *gacchantam na nivarayet*. This is the best way to experience life.

Beyond States

The experience of *turiya* is when you abide in your Self as infinite blissful Consciousness. What is exactly the *turiya* experience? While playing roles you don't forget your nature and remain in blissful consciousness. If, remembering your original nature, you can go through the corridor of waking, dream, sleep and death, then you are in *samadhi*; you are in the state of *turiya*.

Your experience is of different worlds. To begin with, it is the sensate world – the grossest world of creation – *bhautikam*. The second is *annamaya*, the physical body, the instrument and field of experience. The third is *pranamaya*, the physiological system. The fourth world is the psychological – *manomaya*. The fifth world is that of the intellect, *vijnanamaya*, consisting of concepts and ideas. *Anandamaya* is a world beyond *vijnanamaya*, the subtle world of pleasure – the pleasures that you get out of desirable experiences or from sleep. You move in and out of all these worlds and levels of experience. When you think of money and power, you hook on to the material world. When you are hungry you attach to your physical body. At the level of *anandamaya* you are immersed in desirable experiences – when you are not worried about your health, when you have no thoughts, when you sleep deeply. *Anandamaya* is the seat of ignorance and *vasanas*, and it is also called the causal body.

The *peak experience*, which Abraham Maslow distinguished, is only at the pleasure level. At the level of pleasure you have no insight into the highest level of *turiya*, which is gained through meditation. After all, pleasure cannot be equated with meditative bliss. When you experience ordinary pleasures – when you eat good food, when you see a movie, when you talk to an interesting person – you temporarily leave your identification with the material world, the physical, the physiological, the psychological, and intellectual spheres and reside at the level of sheer pleasure, the *anandamaya kosa*. But the state of pleasure is very precarious. You can be pulled back by your thoughts. Even an ant bite is enough for you to fall back into your old world with a thud! All these personality structures and levels of experience fall in the domain of *maya*.

The Wheel of Life

All the worlds of experience are within the *pairs of opposites* paradigm. For example, your experience of pleasure will be invariably followed by the experience of pain. It is an inevitable law of *maya*. There cannot be uninterrupted pleasure. Krishna says,

> *Ye hi samsparsa-ja bhoga duhkha-yonaya eva te*
> *ady-antavantah, Kaunteya, na tesu ramate budhah*

"An intelligent man knows that pleasure born of association with a desirable object is invariably followed by pain born of dissociation with the same; present pleasures are seeds of future pain" (*Gita* V.22). Pleasure and pain invariably follow each other. It is like a revolving wheel – *cakravat parivartate*. We move from success to failure or vice versa. You cannot be permanently successful. Even Napoleon had to face failure intermittently. He almost captured the whole of Eurasia but ultimately had to submit in the fields of Waterloo where he met his doom. If you have had extreme pleasure, wait for the pain. It is there, just round the corner. If you have tremendous pain, then wait for pleasure. So, too, success will inevitably be followed by failure. After running a long distance wouldn't you like to sit down and rest for a while? These polar experiences are called the *pairs of opposites* and are a principle of *maya*.

A sound understanding of the working of *maya* helps you strategize in life and avoid being upset and swept off your feet when success and failure suck you into their vortex. You must have an inner resilience to bounce back after a failure. Some of us have that ability to wait patiently for our time. Have patience. When your time comes, you will again bloom.

We find various paradoxes and contradictions in this world. An unhappy man surrounded by comfort is a paradox. An honest person in the company of cheats is a contradiction. Generally, opposites contradict and negate each other. When light comes, darkness has to go. When goodness comes, badness has to disappear. That is a general law – but not in every instance! For example, sometimes good and bad coexist in the same person. Duryodhana is an example. On one side he was a good man and, on the other side, a bad person. When we find contradictions coexisting, we are puzzled. We can't find a causal relationship for their coexistence. We can only call them asymmetric synchronicities, possibilities in *maya*.

The laws of *maya* help us understand our experiences of contradiction and paradox. We can apply these laws to cope with the complexity of the empirical world and to get the best out of our lives.

The First Law of *Maya*

The first law of *maya* is that everything changes. Nothing is permanent in this world. Our bodies undergo change. We need to accept the fact that we age, and are aging. The body has been made to last for a certain period of time. When its vitality is over, when the body no more responds to your needs, it has to disintegrate and drop off.

Both the objective and the subjective worlds change. Both your physical body and your emotions undergo change. Our emotional profile changes with time and place. Our ideas change, too. Even an insignificant experience can change your ideas. A little hope can change your mind. If you are fascinated by something, your whole world changes. For instance, earlier in life you wished to complete your studies and then join your mother's business. Then you met someone, became excited about him and dropped your original plan. The emotional cloud of infatuation had, by then, obstructed your vision and clarity. When clouds of desire rise in the sky of your mind, the sun of clarity is lost. At that time whatever is told to you, you misunderstand. You ran away with your sweetheart against your parents' wishes. Thereafter, your parents become your number one enemy. This experience is a learning process. Later, after several months, you are ready to call up your parents and plead, "Forgive me. You were right. Please come and take me home!" In India parents always sacrifice for their children. But had this happened in America you would have to face the consequences of your decision all by yourself.

So this cycle is *maya*; everything changes. Our physical body, moods, character, ideas and decisions change constantly. Nothing is the same. Rather everything flows. Change is the law of *maya*.

Managing *Maya* with Detachment

What is the value we learn from the understanding that everything changes? How do we cope with *maya*?

We can learn to cope with *maya* by developing detachment. Relate with everything in a detached and observant manner. Don't lose yourself in an experience. Whenever an experience comes, experience it, go through it – but with the full awareness of your blissful nature. Going through your experiences without losing sight of your inner or higher Self is the meaning of detachment.

Detachment is experiencing without your Self being lost in the experience. It is like taking a bath in the Ganges. How do you take a bath in the Ganges? Currents in the Ganges are very powerful and the round stones on the river bottom are slippery. If, with your ponderous weight, you tiptoe into the Ganges the current will easily carry you off – and you get a free lift to the ocean! To prevent slipping you have to hold onto the ropes tied to the fixed pillars. Holding onto the rope, you have to slowly, firmly and carefully step onto the stones into the river. As long as you hold onto the rope the current will flow without carrying you downstream. Holding onto the rope, you can stay in the midst of the current as long as you wish and have a refreshing bath.

Holding onto your nature, not slipping on the slimy objects, not seeking security from relationships, is the way to cope with *maya*. When you don't seek security and happiness outside, you will be able to experience happiness and security within yourself and enjoy this world to the hilt.

Patanjali says, *Purusasya bhogapavargartham prakrti* – "*Prakrti* is for your enjoyment" (*Yoga Sutras*. II.18). It is like seeing a movie. But when you see a movie you don't identify with it. When there is a winter scene in a cinema, will you take a blanket and cover yourself? You don't because you know what you see is only a movie. This is called detached enjoyment. At the same time, if you don't enjoy your experience, the experience will turn into a bad memory or the memory of a lost opportunity and will unnecessarily take up brain space. Lack of fulfillment often leads to frustration. Frustrations lead to perversion. We should detach and *then* enjoy. Upset and attached you will not enjoy anything. According to Patanjali, everything is for your enjoyment; but you should know *how* to enjoy.

Detach and Transcend

From the law of change, what we understand is the necessity to be detached. Neither run away from situations nor cling unto situations! Be detached. Be detached and then enjoy. When you enjoy with detachment, every experience becomes transcendence. Then you can see the Lord peeping through everything, through different *namarupa* – name and form – whether it is a blooming flower, or a smooth shiny pebble, a twinkling star or a smiling baby. We aspire for the experience of transcendence, the ultimate experience of *moksa*. The ability to go through your experiences holding on to your true nature is *moksa*.

When you apply the value of detachment and enjoy the world, realizing that everything changes, then every experience becomes transcendence. Every enjoyment becomes a window opening to the ultimate, to go beyond. You don't have to be in a cave in the Himalayas waiting for delusions created by the lack of oxygen and call it *samadhi*! You can experience *samadhi* while interacting – while fully alert and alive – in this world. It is in that aliveness that you capture the beautiful face of the Lord, a sense of total oneness and fulfillment, and know the meaning of the phrase, 'One in the many'. Then the whole of life becomes a continuous transcendence. Windows to Heaven open constantly.

The Second Law of *Maya*

The second law of *maya* is the law of interdependence. Everything is interdependent. For instance a particular experience of speaking and listening is possible because the speaker and the listener come together in a common space. Otherwise it could not happen. Such an event happens when two desires coalesce – the speaker's desire to express and the listener's desire to know. It is an interdependent phenomenon. Everything in nature is interdependent, be it a family, an entire country or even a single tree. A tree is not possible without its seed, water, oxygen and sunlight. All these factors together bring the phenomenon of the tree.

The world is so much fused together. Nothing can be independent in this world; everything overflows into everything else. Like a tapestry, where no thread can be removed, nor can one be added. It is a tight and closely-knit interdependent world. The ecological balance is such that if you cut down the rain forests of Indonesia, Malaysia or Brazil, you disturb the ecology of the world. The world is such an integrated web that a local phenomenon becomes a global experience. If the industrialized world were to raise the global temperature even a few degrees, all the icebergs that have existed for millennia will start melting and increase the oceanic level by twenty feet, submerging all major coastal cities including Chennai, Mumbai, New York and Los Angeles!

Life is an interdependent phenomenon. We need harmony between the various levels. We need harmony at home, between our thoughts and feelings, between our words and deeds. No individual exists independent in this closely-knit global tapestry. It simply is not possible to exist independently.

Synergizing Interdependence Through Values

Everything is interdependent. The value we derive out of this understanding is that of *give* and *take*. We must first give in order to later take. We depend upon the other and others depend upon us.

This exchange of energy is called synergy. Synergy creates affluence. So your existence is dependent on the rest of the world; you have to love the whole of humanity.

In the *Gita* there is a concept called *yajna karma*. *Yajna* means "a life of togetherness." Once, the hands picked a quarrel with the stomach because the gossipy mouth told the hands that the stomach enjoyed all the food, and had no work, while the hands had all the work and no food! So, the mouth pointed out that either the stomach should work or the hands should cease working. When the stomach came to know this conversation, it gave a belly laugh and kept quiet. The enraged hands refused to put food into the mouth to teach the stomach a lesson. They went on strike. The stomach was happy because it wanted rest from overeating. The wiley mouth also remained idle. After a half a dozen days, the hands were the first to realize the effect of their "tools down" strike and to understand the truth that what goes into the stomach comes back as nourishment for the whole body, including the hands. That was a valuable lesson in *yagna karma* – the life of interdependence.

Since everything is interdependent we need to practise the value of give and take. Mere understanding of the law of interdependence is not enough. We have to create a value system. We need to create a culture. We must create institutional structures and an environment that promotes these values. When we apply this value we can create affluence:

> *Yatra yog'esvarah Krsno yatra Partho dhanur-dharah*
> *tatra srir vijayo bhutir dhruva nitir matir mama*

"Wherever there is God and man together, there is wealth, continued prosperity, justice, and success" (*Gita* XVIII.78).

What else do we need in life?

The Third Law of *Maya*

The third law of *maya* is the law of balance and equilibrium. The world exists in a delicate and dynamic balance of *sattva*, *rajas* and *tamas* – the good, the active and the dull. If we examine our life, we see that it is a dynamic equilibrium of these three energies. In the morning, since you had a very restful sleep, you are very peaceful and your energy is high. In the morning you look like a god! But by forenoon, when you drive to the office amidst the noisy traffic and pollution, your *rajas* is dominant. You start shouting and screaming at the other drivers. And, by the time you reach the office, *tamas* dominates you. Amidst the mountains of files, you fall asleep!

We need all the three *gunas* in equilibrium. It is in response to bodily and environmental needs that each *guna* comes to predominate the psychic equilibrium. We need to move from *sattva* to *tamas*, to *rajas*, to *tamas* and back to *sattva*. When we fall asleep, *tamas* is dominant. If there is no *tamas* then you will not be able to sleep. You become hyperactive. When we are active, *rajas* manifests. Don't invoke *sattva* at that time. *Sattva* is best invoked in situations where you need compassion, reflection and wisdom

The *gunas* of *sattva*, *rajas* and *tamas* are to be invoked in appropriate situations. Mahatma Gandhi, Buddha, Sri Rama and Christ became active when situations demanded them to be active. They also invoked *sattva* when it was necessary. If you don't have a balance of the three *gunas* – *sattva*, *rajas* and *tamas* – and go to extremes, you'll go crazy. If there is an overabundance of good, *maya* brings some badness also. If there is too much badness, *maya* brings goodness to balance. If there is too much meditation, introduce more activity. If there is too much activity, introduce meditation. Curb your tendency to go to extremes. In the *Gita* it is said,

> *Yukt'ahara-viharasya yukta-cestasya karmasu*
> *yukta-svapn'avabodhasya yogo bhavati duhkha-ha*

"Moderation and the proper blending of everything is that which creates a balance" (VI.17). Too much of anything disturbs balance and causes danger. Even nectar in excess is poison. Be aware of the fluctuations, flow with the flow. With timely interventions, direct the flow of energy towards worthy goals.

Maintaining Equilibrium through Moderation

Moderation, *mitatva*, is a value. Indulging in extremes makes one crazy. There are people whom we call perfectionists, who always want perfection. Since they want perfection, they don't do anything! There are people who say that they don't wish to hurt anybody. So they don't make any decisions! If you are a decisive leader, you may have to hurt a few people. Two values may come in conflict. Say that you worked for twenty-five years and never hurt anyone during your entire career. It not only means that you are a good person, but also *good for nothing*! The meaning of moderation is: when you have to be angry you show anger; when it is necessary to demonstrate your authority and power, you must do that but where mildness is required, then be mild. You must be sensitive to know where and when it is appropriate to express your emotions, your anger, compassion, fear, etc.

You can play with your emotions. Use emotions as tools, but use them intelligently. You should know not only how to get into anger but also to how to relinquish anger. It is easy to get angry – leading to a slippery slope of violent temper and heedless action. Finally, you find yourself in the hospital. You don't know how to get out of your anger. For example, Arjuna's son, Abhimanyu, knew how to penetrate the Kauravas' military formation but did not know how to exit and was brutally killed as a consequence. This felicity, this nimbleness to move in and move out, is the value that we need to cultivate – the value of *mitatva*, moderation. So the value of moderation is summed up as don't go to extremes; don't pursue absolute goodness or badness. This is the meaning of the *Gita* concept of *mitatva* and the Buddhist notion of the golden mean.

In the *Bhagavad Gita* Krishna says that extreme *tapas* is not good. When you do extreme *tapas* God is tortured too (*Gita* XVII.6). Follow the golden mean of moderation. In following the path of moderation you create beauty. Wherever you are, beauty will adorn you. After all, what is beauty? It is blending different things in proportion – a tasty dish, a fine painting, a sturdy house, a well- made garment – anything you create, a blend of various colors and streams proportionately. Nothing goes to extreme – unless it's modern art! When the mind is disturbed – coming from a disturbed family or a violent city – then you just throw colours onto a surface without any meaning or proportional beauty. The chaos thrown on the canvas only represents inner confusion. Of course, to that extent, it is good – at least you know that you are confused.

Beauty is a result of measure and proportion. The ultimate beauty is the character of a person – a Gandhi or a Socrates or a Christ or a Buddha – the harmony of emotions, thoughts, words and conduct. Beauty is a harmonious blend.

Satyam, Shivam, Sundaram

When we apply a system of values to life, these are the three outcomes – transcendence, goodness and beauty or *satyam, shivam, sundaram*. These values should be based upon the proper understanding of the laws of *maya*. *Maya* is a very important tool. Understand what *maya* is. Don't claim, "Everything is *maya*," and continue to sleep. I am reminded of a temple I once visited. Rags and cigarette butts were scattered around the *sanctum sanctorum*. The surrounding yard had long, uncut grass. I asked the priest, "Why don't you keep the temple premises clean? He replied with a question, "Don't you know, everything is *Brahman*?" Logically, he was correct. There is nothing intrinsically wrong with the rags or uncut grass, but they were all in the wrong place. Hair on your head is all right, but if it falls into your food it is repulsive!

We should not resort to an insensitive, irresponsible and callous interpretation of *maya*. *Maya* calls upon us to be ready for change, to be alert, to be creative and not to be pretentious. Through its kaleidoscopically changing structures, *maya* prepares the ground for *Brahman* – our Infinite Potential – to unfold in a rich variety of aesthetic expressions. *Maya* is the facilitator of your unfoldment.

Eight

The Ecstasy of Meditation

SAMADHI

Paradise is now, or never.

Anonymous

As individuals living in a world of constant change we often feel unsettled, stressed and alienated. Rudderless and fearful, feeling lost in a ruthless world, life becomes a melancholic procession of endless sorrows. Like a log of wood drifting down a river, we feel we are being pushed hither and thither by some external power. Our wisdom tradition prescribes the daily practice of meditation as a way out of this mess, as a way to recover our wholeness and to re-establish in the Self. In this dialogue we will discuss the meaning of meditation, the meditator, and the process of meditation.

Meditation and Meaning

Meditation becomes meaningful only when we have an idea about the three factors involved in the practice of meditation, namely:

1) the objective of meditation;
2) the nature of the subject engaged in meditation; and
3) the psycho-physical instruments involved in meditation.

Unless there is clarity about the meditator, the meditated upon and the instruments of meditation, our attempt to meditate becomes difficult, uninspired, confusing and unproductive. This clarity is gained through *sravana* – by attentive listening. Listening to masters of wisdom one gets a clear picture of these three factors. We come to know who we are, what our place is in this world, and about our relationship with God, the Creator.

Three Worldviews

There are three fundamental worldviews that explain our tri-partite existence – the interconnectivity between individuals, the world and God. These worldviews are: Advaita Vedanta, Dvaita Vedanta and the Bauddha Vedanta[1]. Vedanta is a generic word indicating ultimate knowledge. These three worldviews hold different conceptions of God, the individual and of the world. The worldviews of the great Semitic religions – Christianity, Islam

---

The word "Vedanta" is used in the etymological sense of the "end of knowledge or absolute knowledge." Bauddha Vedanta refers to the Buddhist concept of "absolute knowledge."

and Judaism – come under that of Dvaita Vedanta. According to these religions and Dvaita Vedanta, the individual is different from God, the world and other individuals. Advaita Vedanta upholds the unity of all three categories of existence, whereas Buddhism teaches the emptiness of all three concepts.

Meditation and Dvaita Vedanta

Dvaita means "two" or "division." The dvatic meditator begins with the notion of separation from God. God, the world and the individual are co-eternal. In Dvaita Vedanta, the effort is to meditate upon a transcendental and objective God to forget this impermanent and fleeting world of pain and sorrow. The dvaitic meditator tries to constrict his thoughts about the world, keeping them at a bare minimum. Ideally, he thinks about the world only when biological needs arise and, the rest of the time, he spends in contemplation of God. His thought, even while he attends to his biological needs, will be that, "By God's grace, I am able to fulfill these needs."

In the tradition of Dvaita Vedanta, the meditator's attention is focused upon a deity who is all-powerful, who has created the world, who is the paragon of all virtues, and who has compassion for the devotee. The deity could be Krishna, Rama, Jesus Christ, Lakshmi, Narayana, Buddha, Shiva, Sakti, etc. Even a flame, or a flower, the ocean, the sun, fire, breath, or *guru*, etc., could serve as the deity. You can meditate on whatever inspires your heart, or upon whatever your *guru* has suggested for you, or on the *mantra* to which you were given during initiation.

Through the chanting of a *mantra* and meditation you will be able to remember and reestablish your relationship with God. You will be able to submit yourself to the Creator. When your worldly sojourn is over, you go back to the deity of your worship. This is the idea of *salokyam* – the living with God of Dvaita Vedanta. This idea gives you solace and comfort and the hope that, after your physical death, you can go to the world of your deity. During your life in the mortal world, you prepare yourself and purify yourself for the devotional service you will be doing after you join God. Once you go to the world of God, whether it be *Vaikunta* or *Kailasa*, you will be staying there permanently unless you are again sent back to the mortal world on some mission. This is the essential view of Dvaita Vedanta and Vishista Advaita.

The worldview of Christianity is similar to that of Dvaita. Christians believe that Christ died on the cross to atone for mankind's original sin. Man's original sin was the defiance of God. As a result man was expelled from the garden of effortless ease. Now, having been expelled, he has to sweat and toil, live "by the sweat of thy brow." With faith in the sacrifice of Jesus Christ, the only Son of God, the man who repents of his sin attains Heaven in the afterlife.

Meditation and Advaita Vedanta

According to the worldview of Advaita Vedanta, neither the individual nor the world is separate from God. The One Reality, that is Infinite Consciousness, manifests as God, the individual and the world:

Jagat trayam sambhavanartanastali
natadhiraj'otra-parah siva svayam
sabha nata ranga iti vyavasthitih
svarupatah saktiyutat prayuktatah

"All the Three Worlds are Shiva's dancing ground: the dancer, the stage and the spectators are manifestations of the energy of Shiva. All that you see is a spark of that Oceanic Intelligence." God is the organizing principle of the world. Even when you meditate, you understand that the chosen deity on whom you meditate *and* that the mind by which you meditate are both manifestations of that same Reality.

According to Advaita Vedanta, meditation is not just focusing on a particular deity. Focusing upon a particular deity involves choice-making, implies exclusivity, and creates internal conflict. It is like trying to focus your attention on a single dark dot among many on a white screen. As you focus on one or a few allied black dots, your attention has to integrate all the dots *and* the white screen. Then meditation is comprehensive, choice-less, inclusive and conflict-free. There is absolute peace in that holistic meditation. The problem of struggling to keep away dissimilar thoughts – thoughts other than those of your chosen deity, as in the case of dvaitic meditation – does not arise in the advaitic meditation practice. Everything has a place in Consciousness, and nothing can displace Consciousness.

And through meditation we identify ourselves with that borderless Consciousness.

Emptiness and Fullness

A third worldview is that of Buddhism. The Buddha says that everything is *sunya*. All forms, in reality, are emptiness. Your individuality is emptiness. It appears in a certain form, but in reality it is emptiness. It is like peeling off the layers of an onion. What remains when you have peeled off an onion is nothing but a few tears. If you go into the heart of form, there is nothingness. As an individual, you are emptiness; the world is emptiness, and God also is emptiness. Everything – subjective or objective, material or invisible – is pure emptiness.

Buddhist meditation is seeing the emptiness in the form. When you see a flower, what confronts you is a certain pattern. But that pattern has no reality at all. It is only a pattern. It is like waving a burning incense stick in darkness. When you wave the incense stick, it creates empty patterns.

So, our ability to see emptiness in the form is considered meditation. According to Buddha, all our experiences are structures of Consciousness that appear and disappear. So, too, the whole world, our own idea about ourselves, and our idea of God – all these are structures. On the contrary, Vedanta says all that we experience are structures *in* Consciousness, and when structures disintegrate Consciousness remains. What Buddha says is that there are *only* structures. Consciousness is also just a structure. When you see a form, you must equally be able to see formlessness. For the Buddhist formlessness is Emptiness; for the Adviatin formlessness is Fullness.

Non-Judgmental Awareness

What you have to do in meditation is just be aware. This is called *vipasana* in Buddhism and *saksibhava* in Advaita Vedanta. *Asana* means "to remain," and *vipasana* means "to remain without any conclusion." *Saksibhava* is reaction-free witnessing. Both terms indicate the same idea in practice. Generally we make conclusions. Thoughts are conclusions, judgments and comparisons. If you remain without your mind making any conclusions like, "This is good," "This is bad," "This is desirable," or "This is undesirable," then you are in *vipasana* or *saksibhava*. Conclusions are structures that you create in Consciousness. If you can remain absorbed without conclusions, then you are in meditation.

According to Vedanta, in meditation you remain the blissful Self, without any distracting thoughts. Meditation is an enduring state, the pivot of transient experiences. Vedanta asks you to watch as structures form as thoughts. Structures may or may not be there, but watchfulness continues. When the mind's thought-waves are quiet, the Oceanic Consciousness alone exists.

According to Buddhism, at the heart of all experiences is emptiness. The dvaitin sees the beatific face of his Lord at the centre of the world. In Dvaita *sampradaya* (tradition) meditation is called *upasana*. *Upa* means "near," and *asana* means "to sit" – that is, to sit near God. Seeing Emptiness is called *nirvana* in Buddhism. Seeing Fullness is called *prajnasamadhi* or *aparoksa anubhuti* in Advaita Vedanta. And seeing the Lords' beatific face is dvaita *upasana*.

Integral Meditation

For the modern man's meditation, all these three streams of spiritual traditions need to be integrated. You must be able to focus upon an inspiring theme (*upasana*). A meditator has to develop the ability to concentrate on some inspiring idea. We do have the ability to concentrate – we concentrate on the television for eight hours, on rock music or on liquor. But this kind of concentration is misdirected. If I ask you to meditate on a fashion model, you might be able to meditate quite well, but where will it lead you?

We do have the power of concentration, but our minds are unable to concentrate upon uplifting ideals. If I ask you to concentrate on a *Bhagavad Gita* lecture, you might not be able to concentrate for long! If I ask you to meditate on Sarasvati, the goddess of knowledge, you only blink and feel bored. You may concentrate upon Her for some time and then your mind starts wandering. Meditation requires the ability to gather your mind from dissipating and distracting thoughts and focus upon an ennobling idea?

Concentration upon a higher theme integrates body and mind, emotion and imagination, ideas and deeds. Such pursuits make you feel good. A lower theme is that, working on which, you eventually feel disintegrated. Any ideal or pursuit that uplifts you, giving you the experience of integration, wholeness and health, is called concentration. You concentrate upon a chosen ideal. Patanjali's term for this is *dharana*.

Dharana: Concentration for Integration

Dharana is concentrating upon a chosen theme. It is an exclusive activity. Mind does not wander here and there. Mind focuses on one thing. It can concentrate upon God's image or on fixing the morning breakfast or on driving. But don't think of *Brahman* when you drive – that might be fatal! While driving, you have to concentrate upon driving – the road, the gears, the foot pedal, the steering wheel, your speed, the traffic, pedestrians and the policeman!

Any activity that can command concentration is an uplifting activity. If you are unable to concentrate, this inability dissipates your energy. You may concentrate on a mathematical problem. You may concentrate on the star-studded night sky. You may concentrate on any theme that interests to you. Unless we develop the ability of concentration, our meditation will not move into deeper levels.

You have to create the habit of concentration. The *Gita* says,

> *Buddhiyukto jahati'ha ubhe sukrta-duskrte*
> *tasmad yogaya yujyasva yogah karmasu kausalam*

"Work with concentration and work for concentration. Concentration is achieved when you pursue excellence in work, disregarding success or failure" (II.50). Don't think that since you are a failure in life you can easily become a meditator or a *sannyasi*. That is a false notion. The first step in the art of meditation is developing the power of concentration. This power comes when you undertake an activity in the pursuit of a cherished ideal.

Dhyana: Continuous Concentration

It could happen your concentration sags and you become distracted. Therefore one has to practice concentration for a long period of time with deep interest. Patanjali calls this practice *dhyanam* or "continuous concentration."

From *dharana* comes *dhyanam*. And from *dhyana* comes the experience of fusion between you, the one who concentrates, and the object upon which you concentrate. The gap between you and the object is closed, and that experience is *samadhi*. For instance when you are listening to me, you are just listening to me. You have no other thoughts. There is no difference between what you listen to and your mind. Your mind fuses with ideas that you hear. They become the form of your mind. In this state you can say that you have attained total concentration. Patanjali calls this, *Svarupa sunyamiva arthamatra nirbhasam*, that is, "the pursuit without the pursuer" (*Yoga Sutras*. III.3). The object of concentration alone remains as a flame of understanding – a very enjoyable state.

Meditation and Activity

When people come to me to learn meditation, I always ask them whether they have any problem in the office or at home, or, if the seeker is a student, whether he is studying well. If their answer is that they are unable to concentrate, I ask them first to concentrate on their respective work. Doing one's work to the best of one's ability is the starting point of meditation.

Often we see a dichotomy between meditation and activity. We choose to either meditate or work. In fact, meditation is not opposed to activity. There is no division between the two. Arjuna wanted to meditate all the time. He questions Lord Krishna,

> *Jyayasi cet karmanas te mata buddhir, Janardana*
> *tat kim karmani ghore mam niyojayasi, Kesava*

"O Lord, if according to you, meditation is superior to activity, why do you push me into this terrible battle? Why don't you turn the chariot towards the Himalayas, where I can stay and meditate?" (*Gita* III.1). Krishna responded, "Arjuna, your mind will be compulsively thinking of the war. You will never be able to meditate in the Himalayas where you will only be escaping from your duties."

Contextual Concentration

The first lesson we have to learn – if you want to be a real meditator – is the art of concentration on a chosen ideal. And, that is possible only when you are in the midst of activities. You cannot shut your eyes and meditate all your life. If you say that you meditate all the time it only means that you are always sleeping!

The nature of mind is to move from object to object.

> *Cancalam hi manah Krsna pramathi balavad drdham*
> *tasy'aham nigraham manye vayor iva suduskaram*

"The mind is fickle, turbulent and stubborn. To control such a mind is as difficult as stopping a storm" (*Gita*. VI.34). When you try to concentrate, the problems of your mind show up. *Then* you become aware of the structure of mind, its drives, dispositions and conditions. Then you understand the follies and foibles of your mind. It is only when you try to focus that you come to know the degree of distraction that your mind entertains.

The tendency of the mind is to wander around an object and integrate all experiences related to that object. That is how the mind comprehends. Such an integrating enterprise is not opposed to meditation. You should not feel disturbed when the mind wanders from object to object. By cultivating detachment the same wandering mind becomes versatile and integrated.

Detached Concentration

The second quality expected of a meditator is the ability to detach and to see the golden thread that connects seemingly dissimilar objects and contradictory events. The meditator finds a place for all kinds of thoughts in relation to the object of his concentration. This is called detached concentration. Try to integrate your thoughts, locating them in relationship to your central thought, which is God or anything inspiring. When you practice detached concentration, you will be able to focus, withdraw your focus, to command and dismiss thoughts at will. This way the meditator sees the whole picture from a vantage point of detachment. Your mind, like a video camera, focuses upon particular episodes later organizing these experiences into one coherent whole.

Using detached concentration, you are able to concentrate on an object without losing sight of the context. This is also called "contextual concentration". When you see a flower, just seeing the flower is not enough. You must see the flower dancing in the breeze against the background of lush foliage. When you see the flower in the totality, the flower will gain a depth, the surrounding chaos becomes meaningful and your mind ecstatic.

In the process of detached concentration you witness the mind moving from object to object. This process opens a space between you and the witnessing mind. That space allows you enough freedom to command the mind and use it as an effective instrument of pursuing worthy objectives.

Visvarupa Darsana

Detached concentration is called contemplation or reflection. The meaning of *tem* is "to cut off." Contemplation is watching from a distance and not getting lost in the process. When the mirror reflects it does not interpret the object. When you look in the mirror what you see, to a large extent, is true to your real face. The mirror does not interpret your face. If you had a mirror that interpreted your face would you use that mirror? The mirror needs to give a non-judgmental presentation for you to enjoy its use. If the mirror forms an opinion about your face then it is no longer a mirror!

In detached concentration, the mind becomes tolerant,

accommodative and quiet while you are interacting. It is easy to experience quietude when you don't interact, but that deceptive quietude is equivalent to sleep! In sleep mind is quiet, but it is not alert. It is not encompassing. During sleep the mind's full potential is not utilized. Sleep is not meditation.

By detached concentration you reflect the world, see the world in its true nature. When you are able to interact with the world and concentrate at will, with a detached frame of mind, then your mind will remain absolutely quiet without getting disturbed in all your interactions. Your mind will gain clarity while it is interacting with and involved in the world. This state is mystically expressed as the *Visvarupa Darsana*. It is integral experience gained through detached concentration while interacting with the world. Your mind gains the state of *yoga*, the state of cosmic vision described in the *Gita*:

> *Yogasthah kuru karmani sangam tyaktva, Dhananjaya*
> *siddhy-asiddhyoh samo bhutva samatvam yoga ucyate*

"May you perform all your actions endowed with a non-reacting mind, detached from the fruits of work. Yoga is equanimity of mind" (*Gita* II.48).

Samadhi, the Final Gift

Detachment and concentration go together. When you develop these two abilities – to concentrate and to detach – your depths manifest, your spiritual dimension unfolds. You will be led into the inner chambers of ecstasy. This state is described in the *Gita* as

> *Sruti-vipratipanna te yada sthasyati niscala*
> *samadhav acala buddhih tada yogam avapsyasi*

"When your mind is not disturbed and wobbled by the information it receives, when it knows how to stay rooted and respond creatively, then you are in *samadhi*" (II.53). *Samadhi* is being rooted in your spiritual dimension: *Samadhiyate asmin iti samadhi.* Etymologically, *samadhi* means, "That reality, that state unto which everything converges and from which everything emerges."

Samadhi is a gift, not an act. It just happens. Patanjali calls it a "showering of blessings" – *Dharma megha samadhi*. You experience the showering of blessing like snow falling on mountaintops. Something profound overpowers you making you feel blessed. When there is the arousal of inner energies in your interactions, in that state you can say, "I am fulfilled"; "I am filled by that inner dimension"; "I am happy." *Samadhi* is a state of bliss – *Duhkha-samyoga-viyogam yoga-samjnitam* – "*Yoga* is the final dissolution of suffering" (*Gita* VI.23). The experience of unfolding your inner spiritual infinitude through a quiet, mature mind – while interacting with the world – is the ultimate meaning of *samadhi*. It is not a static but a dynamic process. *Samadhi* is Self-Unfoldment in an interactive world.

Appendix of Quotations
from the
Bhagavad Gita

अर्जुन उवाच ।
कार्पण्यदोषोपहतस्वभावः
पृच्छामि त्वां धर्मसंमूढचेताः ।
यच्छ्रेयः स्यान्निश्चितं ब्रूहि तन्मे
शिष्यस्तेऽहं शाधि मां त्वां प्रपन्नम् ॥ II.7 ॥

Arjuna uvaca:
Karpanya-dos'opahata-svabhavah
prcchami tvam dharma-sammudha-cetah /
yac chreyah syan niscitam brvhi tan me
sisyas te' ham sadhi mam tvam prapannam //

Arjuna said, 'My mind deluded by limited understanding, uncharacteristically confused and unable to make the right choices, I beseech Thee to tell clearly what is good for me. I take refuge in Thee; I am Thy disciple. Please teach me!'

श्रीभगवानुवाच ।
अशोच्यानन्वशोचस्त्वं प्रज्ञावादांश्च भाषसे ।
गतासूनगतासूंश्च नानुशोचन्ति पण्डिताः ॥ II.11 ॥

Sri Bhagavan uvaca:
Asocyan anvasocas tvam prajna-vadams ca bhasase /
gat'asun agat'asums ca n'anusocanti panditah //

Lord Krishna said, 'You are grieving for those for whom you need not grieve. Wise men, those who have Self-knowledge, neither grieve for the dead nor for the living.'

यं हि न व्यथयन्त्येते पुरुषं पुरुषर्षभ ।
समदुःखसुखं धीरं सोऽमृतत्वाय कल्पते ॥ II.15 ॥

Yam hi na vyathayanty ete purusam purus'arsabha /
sama-duhkha-sukham dhiram so'mrtatvaya kalpate //

'O Arjuna, bull among men! Only an equanimous person, who remains unaffected by the pairs of opposites—pleasure and pain, and the like—is fit for immortality.'

कर्मण्येवाधिकारस्ते मा फलेषु कदाचन ।
मा कर्मफलहेतुर्भूर्मा ते सङ्गोऽस्त्वकर्मणि ॥ II.47 ॥

Karmany ev'adhikaras te ma phalesu kadacana /
ma karma-phala-hetur bhur ma te sango'stv akarmani //

'You have the right to initiate action, but no control over the outcome. Neither think that you are the author of the results of action nor become attached to idleness.'

योगस्थः कुरु कर्माणि सङ्गं त्यक्त्वा धनंजय ।
सिद्ध्यसिद्ध्योः समो भूत्वा समत्वं योग उच्यते ॥ II.48 ॥

Yogasthah kuru karmani sangam tyaktva, Dhananjaya /
siddhy-asiddhyoh samo bhutva samatvam yoga ucyate //

'O Arjuna, winner of wealth, having renounced attachment to the results of your actions, established in *yoga* (non-reaction), undertake all activities with a steady mind in both success and failure.'

बुद्धियुक्तो जहातीह उभे सुकृतदुष्कृते ।
तस्माद्योगाय युज्यस्व योगः कर्मसु कौशलम् ॥ II.50 ॥

Buddhiyukto jahati'ha ubhe sukrta-duskrte /
tasmad yogaya yujyasva yogah karmasu kausalam //

'A person endowed with equanimity renounces reaction to the outcome of good and bad deeds. For the cultivation of this attitude, engage in activity. Indeed, dexterity in action is non-reaction.'

श्रुतिविप्रतिपन्ना ते यदा स्थास्यति निश्चला ।
समाधावचला बुद्धिस्तदा योगमवाप्स्यसि ॥ II.53 ॥

Sruti-vipratipanna te yada sthasyati niscala /
samadhav acala buddhih tada yogam avapsyasi //

'When intellect, which is disturbed by the external world, comes to steadily and unwaveringly abide in the Self (*samadhau*), then you have attained *yoga*.'

अर्जुन उवाच ।
स्थितप्रज्ञस्य का भाषा समाधिस्थस्य केशव ।
स्थितधीः किं प्रभाषेत किमासीत व्रजेत किम् ॥ II.54 ॥

Arjuna uvaca:
Sthita-prajnasya ka bhasa samadhi-sthasya, Kesava /
sthita-dhih kim prabhaseta kim asita vrajeta kim //

Arjuna said, 'Tell me, O Krishna, about the person of steady wisdom, about the one who is rooted in the Self. How does such a person sit, speak and move about?'

श्रीभगवानुवाच ।
प्रजहाति यदा कामान्सर्वान्पार्थ मनोगतान् ।
आत्मन्येवात्मना तुष्टः स्थितप्रज्ञस्तदोच्यते ॥ II.55 ॥

Sri Bhagavan uvaca:
Prajahati yada kaman sarvan, Partha, mano-gatan /
atmany evatmana tustah sthita-prajnas tado'cyate //

Sri Krishna said, 'O Arjuna, when all desires for happiness are renounced and the mind abides completely satisfied *in* the Self *by* the Self, then, alone, is one called 'the man of steady wisdom.'

दुःखेष्वनुद्विग्नमनाः सुखेषु विगतस्पृहः ।
वीतरागभयक्रोधः स्थितधीर्मुनिरुच्यते ॥ II.56 ॥

Duhkhesu anudvigna-manah sukhesu vigata-sprhah /
vita-raga-bhayakrodhah sthita-dhir munir ucyate //

'Without longing for pleasures, unperturbed by painful experiences, free from attachment, fear and anger – such a silent one is 'a man of steady wisdom.'

एषा ब्राह्मी स्थितिः पार्थ नैनां प्राप्य विमुह्यति ।
स्थित्वास्यामन्तकालेऽपि ब्रह्मनिर्वाणमृच्छति ।। II.72 ।।

Esa braahmi sthitih Partha n'ainam prapya vimuhyati /
sthitva'syam antakale'pi brahma-nirvanam rcchati //

'Having attained this identity with Brahman, O Arjun, son of Pritha, one is no longer deluded. Even at the end of Life, if one should come to realize this, he attains the freedom of being *Brahman*.'

अर्जुन उवाच ।
ज्यायसी चेत्कर्मणस्ते मता बुद्धिर्जनार्दन ।
तत्किं कर्मणि घोरे मां नियोजयसि केशव ।। III.1 ।।

Arjuna uvaca:
Jyayasi cet karmanas te mata buddhir, Janardana /
tat kim karmani ghore mam niyojayasi, Kesava //

Arjuna said: 'O Janardana, tormentor of foes, if, in your opinion, knowledge of the Self is superior to the path of action, then why, Lord of Knowledge, do you urge me to perform this terrible deed?'

श्रीभगवानुवाच ।
न मे पार्थास्ति कर्तव्यं त्रिषु लोकेषु किंचन ।
नानवाप्तमवाप्तव्यं वर्त एव च कर्मणि ॥ III.22 ॥

Sri Bhagavan uvaca:
Na me Partha'sti kartavyam trisu lokesu kimcana /
nanavaptam avaptavyam varta eva ca karmani //

Sri Krishna said, 'O Arjuna, son of Pritha, I have no binding duty to perform in all the three worlds—neither in Heaven, nor Earth nor in the Netherworld. I have nothing to gain that I have not already gained; yet I continue to work vigorously.'

स एवायं मया तेऽद्य योगः प्रोक्तः पुरातनः ।
भक्तोऽसि मे सखा चेति रहस्यं ह्येतदुत्तमम् ॥ IV.3 ॥

Sa ev'ayam maya te' dya yogah proktah puratanah /
bhakto'si me sakha c'eti rahasyam hy etad uttamam //

'The same secret and most exalted knowledge of *yoga* that I taught to the Sun-god, I am teaching to you, Arjuna, My devotee and good friend.'

ये यथा मां प्रपद्यन्ते तांस्तथैव भजाम्यहम् ।
मम वर्त्मानुवर्तन्ते मनुष्याः पार्थ सर्वशः ॥ IV.11 ॥

Ye yatha mam prapadyante tams tath'aiva bhajamy aham /
mama vartm'anuvartante manusyah Partha sarvasah //

'O Arjuna, whosoever approaches me by whatsoever means, in the same way, I reveal myself to him. All paths lead to Me.'

ये हि संस्पर्शजा भोगा दुःखयोनय एव ते ।
आद्यन्तवन्तः कौन्तेय न तेषु रमते बुधः ॥ V.22 ॥

Ye hi samsparsa-ja bhoga duhkha-yonaya eva te /
ady-antavantah, Kaunteya, na tesu ramate budhah //

'O Arjuna, pleasures born of contact with sensory objects, having a beginning and an end, are indeed the seeds of sorrow. Wise men do not get lost in such pleasures.'

अनाश्रितः कर्मफलं कार्यं कर्म करोति यः ।
स संन्यासी च योगी च न निरग्निर्न चाक्रियः ॥ VI.1 ॥

Anasritah karma-phalam karyam karma karoti yah /
sa samnyasi ca yogi ca na niragnir na c'akriyah //

Sri Bhagavan said, 'Whoever does his duty without longing for the fruits of action, is known as a *yogi* and a *sannyasi*—not those who avoid their secular and sacred duties.'

आरुरुक्षोर्मुनेर्योगं कर्म कारणमुच्यते ।
योगारूढस्य तस्यैव शमः कारणमुच्यते ॥ VI.3 ॥

Aruruksor muner yogam karma karanam ucyate /
yog'arudhasya tasy'aiva samah karanam ucyate //

'For that seeker, who would learn the art of balancing his mind, it is said that activity is the means. For one who has succeeded in balancing an active mind, subtle efforts in Self-abidance—like *sravana*, *manana* and *nididhyasana*—are said to be the means.'

युक्ताहारविहारस्य युक्तचेष्टस्य कर्मसु ।
युक्तस्वप्नावबोधस्य योगो भवति दुःखहा ॥ VI.17 ॥

Yukt'ahara-viharasya yukta-cestasya karmasu /
yukta-svapn'avabodhasya yogo bhavati duhkha-ha //

'The practice of *yoga* removes afflictions for one who is moderate in both sleep and waking life, moderate in eating, personal conduct and work.'

तं विद्याद दुःखसंयोगवियोगं योगसंज्ञितम् ।
स निश्चयेन योक्तव्यो योगोऽनिर्विण्णचेतसा ॥ VI.23 ॥

Tam vidyad duhkha-samyoga-viyogam yoga-samjnitam /
sa niscayena yoktavyo yogo'nirvinna cetasa //

'*Yoga* is nothing but "dissociation from association with sorrow." Casting despondency aside, this discipline of *yoga* must be practiced with great resolve.'

अर्जुन उवाच ।
चंचलं हि मनः कृष्ण प्रमाथि बलवद् दृढम् ।
तस्याहं निग्रहं मन्ये वायोरिव सुदुष्करम् ॥ VI.34 ॥

Arjuna uvaca:
Cancalam hi manah Krsna pramathi balavad drdham /
tasy'aham nigraham manye vayor iva suduskaram //

Arjuna said, 'The mind is fickle, turbulent, unyielding, and powerful, O Krishna. I think that subduing the mind is as difficult as controlling the wind.'

श्रीभगवानुवाच ।
बलं बलवतां चाहं कामरागविवर्जितम् ।
धर्माविरुद्धो भूतेषु कामोऽस्मि भरतर्षभ ॥ VII.11 ॥

Sri Bhagavan uvaca:
Balam balavatam ca'ham kama-raga-vivarjitam /
dharm'aviruddho bhutesu kamo'smi Bharta'rsabha //

Sri Krishna said, 'O Arjuna, most exalted Prince! In the strong, I am strength free from selfish desire and attachment. In the righteous, I am desire that is unopposed to goodness.'

चतुर्विधा भजन्ते मां जनाः सुकृतिनोऽर्जुन ।
आर्तो जिज्ञासुरर्थार्थी ज्ञानी च भरतर्षभ ॥ VII.16 ॥

Catur-vidha bhajante mam janah sukrtino'rjuna /
arto jijnasur arth'arthi jnani ca Bharata'rsabha //

'O hero among men! Four types of virtuous people seek Me: the distressed; knowledge seekers; wealth and success seekers; and wise men.'

पत्रं पुष्पं फलं तोयं यो मे भक्त्या प्रयच्छति ।
तदहं भक्त्युपहृतमश्नामि प्रयतात्मनः ॥ IX.26 ॥

Patram puspam phalam toyam yo me bhaktya prayacchati/
tad aham bhakty-upahrtam asnami prayat'atmanah //

'Whoever offers a leaf or flower, fruit or water unto Me with pure devotion, I receive those offerings with the same ardour.'

अद्वेष्टा सर्वभूतानां मैत्रः करुण एव च ।
निर्ममो निरहङ्कारः समदुःखसुखः क्षमी ॥ XII.13 ॥

Advesta sarva-bhutanam maitrah karuna eva ca /
nirmamo nirahamkarah sama-duhkha-sukhah ksami //

'With malice towards none, with friendliness and compassion for all, with non-possessiveness and non-doership, ever the same in pain and pleasure, patient and forgiving...such are the qualities of a true devotee.'

अमानित्वमदम्भित्वमहिंसा क्षान्तिरार्जवम् ।
आचार्योपासनं शौचं स्थैर्यमात्मविनिग्रहः ॥ XIII.7 ॥

Amanitvam adambhitvam ahimsa ksantir arjavam /
acary'opasanam saucam sthairyam atma-vinigrahah //

'Humility, modesty, non-violence, patience, straightforwardness, service to the *Guru*, cleanliness, steadfastness and self-control ...' (continued)

इन्द्रियार्थेषु वैराग्यमनहंकार एव च ।
जन्ममृत्युजराव्याधिदुःखदोषानुदर्शनम् ॥ XIII.8 ॥

Indriy'arthesu vairagyam anahamkara eva ca /
janma-mrtyu-jara-vyadhi-duhkha-dos'anudarsanam //

'…with dispassion towards objects of the senses, egolessness (non-doer-ship), acceptance (awareness/accommodation) of the limitations of birth, death, old age, disease and sorrow…'

असक्तिरनभिष्वङ्गः पुत्रदारगृहादिषु ।
नित्यं च समचित्तत्वमिष्टानिष्टोपपत्तिषु ॥ XIII.9 ॥

Asaktir anabhisvangah putra-dara-grhadisu /
nityam ca sama-cittatvam ist'anist'opapattisu //

'…non-attachment and non-identification with children, spouse and home, remaining even-minded when in contact with either desirable or undesirable objects…' (continued)

मयि चानन्ययोगेन भक्तिरव्यभिचारिणी ।
विविक्तदेशसेवित्वमरतिर्जनसंसदि ॥ XIII.10 ॥

Mayi c'ananya-yogena bhaktir avyabhicarini /
vivikta-desa-sevitvam aratir jana-samsadi //

'…unflinching in devotion to Me (The Lord), with the awareness of non-separateness, a love for solitude, avoiding fruitless company and conversation…' (continued)

अध्यात्मज्ञाननित्यत्वं तत्त्वज्ञानार्थदर्शनम् ।
एतज्ज्ञानमिति प्रोक्तमज्ञानं यदतोऽन्यथा ॥ XIII.11 ॥

Adhyatma-jnana-nityatvam tattva jnanartha-darsanam /
etat jnanam iti proktam ajnanam yad ato'nyatha //

'. . .steadiness in Self-Knowledge and realizing the benefit of Self-Knowledge—these twenty values are called Knowledge and anything opposed to these is called ignorance.'

सर्वेन्द्रियगुणाभासं सर्वेन्द्रियविवर्जितम् ।
असक्तं सर्वभृच्चैव निर्गुणं गुणभोक्तृ च ॥ XIII.14 ॥

Sarv'edriya-gun'abhasam sarv'endriya vivarjitam /
asaktam sarva-bhrc c'aiva nirgunam guna-bhoktr ca //

'Consciousness/Brahman is neither conditioned by mind, nor the sense organs nor sense activity and yet illumines them all. Though detached, It supports everything. Enjoying the three *gunas* It remains unaffected by their play.'

कर्षयन्तः शरीरस्थं भूतग्राममचेतसः ।
मां चैवान्तःशरीरस्थं तान्विद्ध्यासुरनिश्चयान् ॥ XVII.6 ॥

Karsayantah sarira-stham bhuta-gramam acetasah /
mam ˆ'aiva'ntah-sarira-stham tan viddhy asura-niscayan //

'Mindless people of evil resolve, who torture their bodies and senses, also torture Me, as I am the Self in them.'

त्याज्यं दोषवदित्येके कर्म प्राहुर्मनीषिणः ।
यज्ञदानतपःकर्म न त्याज्यमिति चापरे ।। XVIII.3 ।।

Tyajyam dosavad ity eke karma prahur manisinah /
yajna-dana-tapah-karma na tyajyam iti c'apare //

'Some sages say that all activities are defective and should be renounced, while others say that three types of activities – *yagna* (altruistic work), *dana* (sharing), and *tapah* (austerities) are *not* to be relinquished.'

यतः प्रवृत्तिर्भूतानां येन सर्वमिदं ततम् ।
स्वकर्मणा तमभ्यर्च्य सिद्धिं विन्दति मानवः ।। XVIII.46 ।।

Yatah pravrttir bhutanam yena sarvam idam tatam /
sva-karmana tam abhyarcya siddhim vindati manavah //

'Worshiping the Lord—the All-Pervading Creator of the world—through their work, people gain spiritual fulfillment.'

सहजं कर्म कौन्तेय सदोषमपि न त्यजेत् ।
सर्वारम्भा हि दोषेण धूमेनाग्निरिवावृताः ।। XVIII.48 ।।

Sahajam karma, Kaunteya, sadosam api na tyajet /
sarv'arambha hi dosena dhumen'agnir iv'avrtah //

'O Arjuna, do not abandon work born of your nature even thought it is imperfect. Just as fire is attended by smoke, all enterprises have their defects.'

संजय उवाच ।
यत्र योगेश्वरः कृष्णो यत्र पार्थो धनुर्धरः ।
तत्र श्रीर्विजयो भूतिर्ध्रुवा नीतिर्मतिर्मम ॥ XVIII.78 ॥

Sanjaya uvaca:
Yatra yog'esvarah Krsno yatra Partho dhanur-dharah /
tatra srir vijayo bhutir dhruva nitir matir mama //

Sanjaya said: 'In my opinion, wherever there is Krishna, the Lord of *Yoga*, and Arjuna, the man of action, there is wealth, success, steady growth and justice.'

Appendix of Quotations
from
Patanjali's *Yoga Sutras*

1. *Sutra* I.48

ऋतंभरा तत्र प्रज्ञा ॥48॥
Rtambhara tatra prajna.

In samadhi knowledge resonates with the rhythm and harmony of existence.

2. *Sutra* II.18

प्रकाशक्रियास्थितिशीलं भूतेन्द्रियात्मकं भोगापवर्गार्थम्
दृश्यम् ॥18॥

Prakasa-kriya-sthitisilam bhutendriyatmakam bhogapavargartham drsyam.

The objective world of senses and sense objects
constituted of the energy of illumination,
activity and inertia – sattva, rajas and tamas –
is for the purpose of enjoyment and transcendence.

3. *Sutra* II.29

यमनियमासनप्राणायामप्रत्याहारधारणाध्यानसमाधयोऽष्टौ
अङ्गानि ॥29॥

Yama niyamasana pranayama pratyahara dharana dhyana samdhayo'stavangani.

The eight limbs of yoga are: *yama* and *niyama*, meaning ethical discipline and moral practices; *asana*, physical discipline; *pranayama*, physiological controls; *pratyahara*, detachment; *dharana*, concentration; *dhyana*, contemplation; and *samadhi*, immersion.

4. *Sutra* III.3

तद् एवार्थमात्रनिर्भासं स्वरूपशून्यम् इव समाधिः ॥3॥

Tad eva'rthamatra-nirbhasam svarupa-sunyam iva samadhih.

Samadhi is perception of reality without egoistic interpretations.

5. *Sutra* IV.28

प्रसंख्यानेऽप्यकुसीदस्य सर्वथाविवेकख्यातेर्धर्ममेघः समाधिः ॥28॥

Prasankhyane'pyakusitasya sarvatha-vivekakhyateh-dharma-megha samadhi.

The shower of virtue falls on him who with the power of discrimination remains undistracted even by psychic powers.

Appendix of Quotations
from the
Upanishads and Other Sources

1. *Isavasya Upanishad*. 5:

तदेजति तन्नैजति तद्दूरे तद्वन्तिके ।
तदन्तरस्य सर्वस्य तदु सर्वस्यास्य बाह्यतः ॥5॥

Tadejati tannaijati taddure tadvantike /
Tadantarasya sarvasya tadu sarvasyasya bahyatah.

It moves and it moves not, it is far and it is near;
it is inside all and outside, too.

2. *Isavasya Upanishad, Mool Mantra*:

ॐ पूर्णमदः पूर्णमिदं पूर्णात् पूर्णमुदच्यते ।
पूर्णस्य पूर्णमादाय पूर्णमेवावशिष्यते ॥
ॐ शांतिः शांतिः शांतिः ॥

Purnam adah purnam idam
purnat purnam udacyate /
purnasya purnam adaya
purnam evavasisyate //

Om shantih, shantih, shantih.

That is complete; this also is complete;
The complete manifests from the complete.
Taking the complete from the complete,
the complete itself remains because
This is non-separate from That.
Om, Peace, Peace, Peace.

3. *Narada Bhakti Sutras*, I.2:

सा त्वस्मिन् परमप्रेमरूपा ॥ 2 ॥

Sa tvasmin paramaprema rupa.

Devotion is unconditional (non-demanding) love for God.

4. *Brhad-aranyaka Upanishad*, IV.v.6:

आत्मनस् तु कामाय सर्वम् प्रियम् भवति ।
आत्मा वा अरे द्रष्टव्यः श्रोतव्यो मन्तव्यो
निदिध्यासितव्यो मैत्रेयि ॥ 6 ॥

Atmanastu kamaya sarvam priyam bhavati.
Atma va are drstavyah srotavyo mantavyo
nididhyasitavyo Maitreyi.

O Maitreyi, it is love for oneself
that makes everything else loveable;
All forms of love are search for the immutable
SELF! Listening, reflecting and meditating on the
Immutable Self is the path to Self-Realization.

5. *Katha Upanishad*, II.i.10:

यदेवेह तदमुत्र यदमुत्र तदन्विह ।
मृत्योः स मृत्युमाप्नोति य इह नानेव पश्यति ॥

Yadeveha tadamutra yadamutra tadanviha /
Mrtyoh sa mrtyum apnoti ya eha naneva pasyati.

The manifest and the unmanifest are the same
Truth, what is 'There,'
That alone is 'Here.' He who sees 'Here' the
many, goes from death to death.

6. Sankaracharya's *Atma Bodha*, 6:

संसार स्वप्नतुल्यो हि रागद्वेषादिसङ्कुलः ।
स्वकाले सत्यवद् भाति प्रबोधे सत्यसद् भवेत् ॥

Samsara svapnatulyo hi ragadvesadisankulah /
svakale satyavadbhati prabodhe satyasad bhavet //

Empirical life is like a dream,
riddled with like, dislike, etc.
In their own time they are real,
but upon waking, become unreal.

Ashrams & Organizations

Swami Bodhananda

Founder & Spiritual Director

Sambodh Foundation

K-11 Kailash Colony
New Delhi, 110 048 India
Tel: (011) 2628 9247

Bodhananda Research Foundation for Management & Leadership Studies Bodhananda Kendra

Kalady, Karamana P.O.
Thiruvananthapuram 695 002
Tel: (0471) 344 084 / 433 084
Email: tvm_brfmldns@sancharnet.in

Bodhananda Seva Society & Bodhananda Kendra

Kalady, Karamana P.O.
Thiruvananthapuram 695 002
Tel: (0471) 344 084 / 433 084

Vrindavan Vanaprastha Ashram

Bodhananda Kendra
Kalady, Karamana P.O.
Thiruvananthapuram 695 002
Tel: (0471) 344 084 / 433 084

Bodhananda Kendra

Kizhakkepattu, Chevarambalam P.O.
Kozhikode 673 017
Tel: (0495) 373 527 / 355 474

Bodhananda Kendra

Puliyathu Mukku, Kilikollur P.O.
Kollam 691 004
Tel: (0474) 718 905 / 719021

Ashraya Training Centre

A Residential School for Handicapped Girl Children
Puliyathu Mukku, Kilikollur P.O.
Kollam 691 004
Tel: (0474) 718 905 / 719 021

Sambodh Foundation

c/o S. Gopalakrishnan
G-190 Sahakara Nagara
Kodigehalli
Bangalore 560 092
Tel: (080) 353 5500

Bodhananda Sruti Seva Trust

Bhadra, 2/594, Vazhakkala, Trikkakara PO
Ernakulum, Cochin 682 021
Tel: (0484) 421 029 / 421 029

The Sambodh Society, Inc.

Dr. Uma Deperalta. M.D., Trustee
7002 N. La Presa Drive
San Gabriel, California 91775
USA
Tel: (626) 292 6883

The Sambodh Society, Inc.

Dr. Ruth Harring, Ph.D., Trustee
USA Program Coordinator
1826 Charter Avenue
Kalamazoo, Michigan 49024
USA
Tel: (616) 327 3774
Email: Indiaink@worldnet.att.net